高职高专旅游英语系列教材

Spoken English for Tourism

旅游英语口语

主　编　戴丽萍　郝立英
副主编　周　迎　张志华

清华大学出版社
北京交通大学出版社
·北京·

内 容 简 介

本书共 8 个单元,是为"旅游英语口语"课程编写的教材。本书的每一个单元均设计有导学、模仿交际、看图说话、角色扮演、即兴对话、问卷调查、采访和辩论等形式相互结合的教学模块。

本书可作为高职高专及远程教育旅游英语及相关专业的教材使用,也可作为旅游职业工作者或旅游爱好者的自学教材和读物。

本书封面贴有清华大学出版社防伪标签,无标签者不得销售。
版权所有,侵权必究。侵权举报电话:010-62782989　13501256678　13801310933

图书在版编目(CIP)数据

旅游英语口语 / 戴丽萍,郝立英主编. — 北京:北京交通大学出版社:清华大学出版社,2020.6(2023.8 重印)
ISBN 978-7-5121-3996-1

Ⅰ. ①旅… Ⅱ. ①戴… ②郝… Ⅲ. ①旅游–英语–口语–教材 Ⅳ. ①F59

中国版本图书馆 CIP 数据核字(2019)第 167890 号

旅游英语口语
LÜYOU YINGYU KOUYU

责任编辑:张利军

出版发行:	清华大学出版社　邮编:100084　电话:010-62776969　http://www.tup.com.cn		
	北京交通大学出版社　邮编:100044　电话:010-51686414　http://www.bjtup.com.cn		

印　刷　者:北京时代华都印刷有限公司
经　　　销:全国新华书店
开　　　本:185 mm×230 mm　　印张:8.75　　字数:196 千字
版 印 次:2020 年 6 月第 1 版　　2023 年 8 月第 2 次印刷
印　　　数:3 001~4 000 册　　定价:38.00 元

本书如有质量问题,请向北京交通大学出版社质监组反映。对您的意见和批评,我们表示欢迎和感谢。
投诉电话:010-51686043,51686008;传真:010-62225406;E-mail:press@bjtu.edu.cn。

"高职高专旅游英语系列教材"编委会

王建荣　　任　淼　　李　辉　　李家坤

张志华　　陈琳琳　　林　昊　　周　迎

周红红　　赵　挺　　郝立英　　戴丽萍

阎　莉　　张雅娜

前言 Preface

改革开放 40 多年来，我国取得了举世瞩目的伟大成就，发生了翻天覆地的变化，而旅游业也以其强劲的势头成为我国经济发展中最具活力的"朝阳产业"。随着改革开放的不断深化，我国的旅游业正面临着前所未有的跨越式发展机遇。无论是国内旅游，还是跨境旅游，其规模越来越大，品种越来越多，层次越来越高，旅游业已从单纯的游玩上升为一种文化性产业。因此，旅游业的不断发展对旅游从业人员的素质要求也越来越高。他们不仅需要丰富的专业知识，而且随着跨境旅游规模的不断扩大，过硬的英语交流能力已成为他们提升竞争力的主要技能。为尽快培养出合格的旅游从业人才，满足旅游市场的需要，促进我国旅游事业的蓬勃发展，编写一套系统而实用的旅游英语教材是十分必要和紧迫的。

为满足我国高职高专院校旅游英语专业教学的迫切需求，适应当前我国旅游业的快速发展，我们组织国内部分高校从事旅游英语教学的骨干教师编写了这套"高职高专旅游英语系列教材"。本系列教材主要包括《旅游英语口语》《旅游英语会话》《旅游英语听力（第 1 册）》《旅游英语听力（第 2 册）》《旅游英语泛读》5 本教材。

本系列教材具有以下特点。

（1）以任务为导向，以交际为主旨。本系列教材配有大量的练习，学练一体，课文内容和练习与现场操作实务密切相关，学生完全能够学以致用，学习效率高。学生不仅可以与其他同学互练，也可以进行自主练习，大量操练语言输出。

（2）选材贴近专业，取材真实广泛。本系列教材的选材均来自地道的旅游方面的原版文章和会话，材料真实，贴近专业，融知识性、真实性和趣味性于一体，学生学起来有兴趣、有动力、效率高。

（3）教材设计科学，互补性强。本系列教材根据高职高专学生的特点设置教学内容，每个单元的学习量适中，简练易学。本系列教材基本涵盖了旅游英语的听、说、读、写功能，能够体现旅游特色和交际功能，从基础口语、专业会话、词汇扩充和专业知识阅读等方面进行了系统的内容安排，使学生能够大幅提升旅游英语综合应用能力。

（4）在娱乐中学习，以兴趣促提高。本系列教材除了在每个单元安排大量实用性强的学习内容之外，还选用了许多能够激发学生学习兴趣的音频和视频资料，如歌曲、语言故事、著名景点介绍和图片等，让学生在娱乐中汲取专业知识，巩固专业基础。

本书为《旅游英语口语》，共8个单元，是为"旅游英语口语"课程编写的教材。

掌握基本的口语是交流的基础，因此本书从日常的基本交流开始，从简单的句型到连续的会话，从日常用语到旅游用语，均做了详尽的设计和安排，学生能在不知不觉中过渡到旅游英语会话阶段。本书的每一个单元均设计有导学热身、模仿交际、看图说话、角色扮演、即兴对话、问卷调查、采访和辩论等教学形式相互结合的教学活动。

为了方便课堂教学和学生自主学习，本书配有学习指导、视频讲解、MP3录音、模拟试题、练习答案等教学资源。学习指导不仅可以指导学生如何进行学习，还就教材的学习内容进行辅导，具体包括学习重点及学习难点、学习目标及学习要求、预备知识、学习课时安排、学习内容及指导、语言归纳及常见错误分析、知识扩展等，是学生自主学习和教师课堂教学不可或缺的辅助材料。视频讲解是针对教材内容的精讲，旨在为学生提供更好的自主学习资源和学习途径。MP3录音为教材中对话、听力练习及其他相关教学内容的配套音频资源，由母语为英语的专业人士配音录制，旨在为学生营造良好的语言学习环境。模拟试题紧密结合教材内容编写而成，在题型设计上充分考虑对学生旅游英语口语交际能力的考查，涉及语言材料广泛，贴近实际工作和生活。练习答案则针对教材中的练习题及模拟试题提供相应的解答。读者可先扫描书后的防盗码获取资源读取权限，然后再扫描书中每单元开始处的二维码来获取相应的教学资源。

本书的主要特色如下。

（1）紧密结合教学改革的课程体系建设和课程内容要求，根据读者对象的特点组织教材的内容。

（2）遵循"实用为主，够用为度"的原则，以培养学生实际口语交际能力为目的，突出教学的实用性和针对性。

（3）通过真实而富有时代气息的场景、地道而生动的语言素材、丰富而实用的表达、活泼而形式多样的练习提高学生在各种旅游场景下的旅游英语口语交际能力。

（4）配备立体化的教学资源，通过文本及音频、视频、动画等多种媒体形式来呈现教学内容，为学生提供可资模仿的旅游英语口语范例，帮助学生完成人际口语交流，同时也方便学生自主学习。

在本书构思、选材、编写、审稿和出版过程中，众多学者和一线工作人员给我们提出了宝贵的意见和建议，同时也得到了编者所在院校及出版社的大力支持。在此，全体编写人员向他们致以诚挚的谢意。

由于编写时间仓促且编写人员水平有限，书中疏漏之处在所难免，欢迎广大读者批评指正。

编　者
2020年5月

Contents

Unit 1	Outdoor Activities	1
Unit 2	Communication	16
Unit 3	Food	32
Unit 4	Shopping	48
Unit 5	Transportation	63
Unit 6	Travel	79
Unit 7	Weather	95
Unit 8	Festival	113

Unit 1 Outdoor Activities

Outdoor activity refers to leisure pursuits in the outdoors, often in natural or semi-natural settings out of town. There are various outdoor activities for different seasons. In spring, people like visiting gardens, climbing mountains and flying kites. In summer, they like swimming, sailing or scuba diving. In autumn, they can camp, cycle or hike. In winter, skiing or ice skating are popular games. What's more, different people pursue different outdoor activities. Old people like walking and jogging. Young people like exciting activities, such as diving, skiing and horse riding, etc.

Learning Objectives

In this unit you are going to:
★ learn some new words related to outdoor activities;
★ learn speaking skills — expressing likes and dislikes;
★ practice speaking around the topics given.

Section I Words and Sentence Patterns

Part I Words Related to Outdoor Activities

You may engage in a lot of outdoor activities in your leisure time. Do you know how to express them in English? Now let's learn some key words related to them.

Land Sports

1. mountain climbing /'maʊntɪn//'klaɪmɪŋ/   登山
2. rock climbing /rɒk//'klaɪmɪŋ/   攀岩
3. bouldering /'bəʊldərɪŋ/   徒手攀岩
4. adventure /əd'ventʃə/   探险
5. hiking /'haɪkɪŋ/   远足
6. camping /'kæmpɪŋ/   露营
7. skydiving /'skaɪˌdaɪvɪŋ/   跳伞运动
8. horse riding /hɔːs//'raɪdɪŋ/   骑马
9. cycling /'saɪkəlɪŋ/   骑自行车
10. jogging /'dʒɒgɪŋ/   慢跑
11. yoga /'jəʊgə/   瑜伽
12. ice skating /aɪs//'skeɪtɪŋ/   溜冰
13. skiing /'skiːɪŋ/   滑雪
14. roller blading /'rəʊlə//'bleɪdɪŋ/   溜旱冰
15. snowboarding /'snəʊˌbɔːdɪŋ/   玩滑雪板
16. skateboarding /'skeɪtˌbɔːdɪŋ/   滑板运动
17. roller coaster /'rəʊlə//'kəʊstə/   过山车
18. desert jeep safari /'dezət//dʒiːp//sə'fɑːrɪ/   沙漠冲沙
19. bungee jumping /'bʌndʒɪ//'dʒʌmpɪŋ/   蹦极
20. barbecue (BBQ) /'bɑːbɪkjuː/   烧烤

Unit 1 Outdoor Activities

Water Sports

1. river tracing /ˈrɪvə//ˈtreɪsɪŋ/ 溯溪
2. rafting /ˈrɑːftɪŋ/ 泛舟
3. canyoning /ˈkænjənɪŋ/ 峡谷漂流
4. swimming /ˈswɪmɪŋ/ 游泳
5. diving /ˈdaɪvɪŋ/ 浮潜
6. scuba diving /ˈskjʊbə//ˈdaɪvɪŋ/ 水肺潜水
7. snorkeling /ˈsnɔːkəlɪŋ/ （戴呼吸器）浮潜
8. beach volleyball /biːtʃ//ˈvɒlibɔːl/ 沙滩排球
9. surfing /ˈsɜːfɪŋ/ 冲浪
10. wind surfing /wɪnd//ˈsɜːfɪŋ/ （风帆）冲浪
11. water skiing /ˈwɔːtə//skiːɪŋ/ 滑水
12. wakeboarding /ˈweɪkbɔːdɪŋ/ （用滑板）滑水
13. canoeing /kəˈnuːɪŋ/ 划独木舟
14. rowing /ˈrəʊɪŋ/ 划船
15. sailing /ˈseɪlɪŋ/ 航海
16. kayaking /ˈkaɪækɪŋ/ 皮划艇运动
17. parasailing /ˈpærəˌseɪlɪŋ/ 帆伞运动
18. kitesurfing /ˈkaɪtˌsɜːfɪŋ/ 风筝冲浪
19. hot spring /hɒt//sprɪŋ/ 温泉
20. dragon boat racing /ˈdrægən//bəʊt//ˈreɪsɪŋ/ 赛龙舟

Part II Sentence Patterns Related to Outdoor Activities

1. **A:** What do you like to do during holidays?
   B: I like hiking in the mountains.
2. **A:** What's your favorite outdoor activity?
   B: I like lots of outdoor activities. But I prefer cycling and running the most.

3. **A:** How often do you play beach volleyball?
   B: I play it once a week.
4. **A:** Why do you like water skiing?
   B: Because it's exciting and relaxing.

Section II Conversations

You may want to be cool when communicating with your friends in WeChat in English. Listen and learn the following conversations.

Conversation 1

A: I'm bored. Do you want to do something?
B: What did you have in mind?
A: The weather is fine for outdoor sports. Exercises taken in open air are contributive to our health.
B: I'm just thinking about the same as you.
A: How about going swimming this weekend?
B: Good idea. That's exactly what I want to do.

Conversation 2

A: What would you do in your free time?
B: Me? I like outdoor activities, I guess.
A: Like sports?
B: Yes. I really like cycling and walking. It keeps me fit and healthy.
A: Yes, they're good for you. I must admit I like walking, too. I go walking in the parks in Beijing most weekends.
B: I like lots of different keep-fit activities like that — most sports, going to the gym, that kind of thing.

Unit 1
Outdoor Activities

Conversation 3

A: Say, what do you like to do in your spare time?
B: I like to play computer games quite a bit.
A: Don't you enjoy hiking?
B: No, I like staying at home and playing games.
A: Oh, that's not good for your health.

Conversation 4

A: Do you like outdoor activities?
B: Yeah, mountain hiking. Other than that, things that I've done and do every once in a while are outdoor swimming, canoeing, kayaking, fishing, snorkeling, camping, boating, and taking pictures outdoors.
A: I heard there are a lot of beautiful mountains famous for hiking. Is that true?
B: That's true. The area where I grew up is actually quite close to a famous mountain in this city. You can go on for a day, or two days, a week, ten days, a month if you want to.

Conversation 5

A: I think there must be a lot of outdoor activities in this city, right?
B: Hmm.
A: Some extreme sports?

B: Right. Yeah, there are so many water sports. People really love water sports because it's tropical warm climate year round. The marine climate is quite warm and at the same time there are a lot of really big waves.
A: Great. I also heard about diving.
B: Ah, yeah. One is shark cage diving that people are really interested in. But I think it is a bit scary.

Section III Practice

I. Complete the following conversation with the phrases given.

> A. I'll go with you
> B. What about you
> C. Have a good time

A: What are you going to do this weekend?

B: I have no idea. 1_____?

A: I'm going to hike and camp in the mountains. There'll be a party.

B: Cool. 2_____!

A: Why not come and join us? We can go dancing and singing.

B: OK. 3_____.

A: Wonderful!

II. Complete the following conversation with the sentences given.

> A. I like it because it's exciting.
> B. Who do you often play tennis with?
> C. I usually watch it on TV.
> D. what are your favorite outdoor activities?
> E. but I guess I like tennis better.
> F. How often do you play tennis?

A: Say, 1_____

B: Hm… it's hard to say. I like basketball a lot, 2_____

A: Why do you like it?

B: 3_____

A: 4_____

B: Once a week.

A: 5_____

Unit 1　Outdoor Activities

B: I often play tennis with my friends. How about a game sometime?
A: Sorry, 6_____

III. Match the items in Column A with the items in Column B.

A	B
1. How often do you go jogging?	A. I like it because it's exciting.
2. What's your favorite outdoor activity?	B. I often go with my friends.
3. Who do you often go hiking with?	C. I usually do it early in the morning.
4. Why do you like sailing?	D. I go jogging every day.
5. When do you usually go cycling?	E. Diving is my favorite.

IV. Work in pairs and discuss the questions: Have you ever tried the following outdoor leisure activities in your spare time? Then check the ones you have never done but long to have a try and give your reasons.

★scuba diving

★kayaking

★skydiving

★parasailing

★camping

★bouldering

★bungee jumping

★snowboarding

★water skiing

★roller coaster

V. Tell your partner what you like doing in your free time and what you're going to do this weekend.

In my free time I enjoy _____, and I love _____ because _____
_____. This weekend I'm going to _____ and _____.

VI. Work in pairs and discuss the following questions.

★ How do you usually spend your weekends?
★ What do you do to relax yourself?
★ What are the most popular outdoor leisure activities in your city?

Section IV Speaking Skills: Expressing Likes or Dislikes

There are many ways of expressing likes and dislikes. Read the following expressions and learn a few of them.

Likes	Dislikes
I like/love reading.	I hate ice skating.
I prefer fishing to swimming.	I don't care for ice cream.
I'm interested in watching TV.	I can't stand/bear/put up with rock climbing.
I enjoy net chatting.	That's the last thing I need.
My favorite sport is sailing.	I'm tired of skydiving.
I'm keen on diving.	I'm fed up with Internet surfing.
I'm fond of visiting museums.	I'm bored to death with camping.
I have fancy of shopping.	I especially dislike bungee jumping.
Do you go in for jogging?	
I'm crazy about water skiing.	

Unit 1 Outdoor Activities

Conduct a survey by using the following form to find out the leisure activities that your classmates like and dislike.

Leisure activities	Love	Like	OK	Dislike	Hate
Go hiking					
Surfing					
Hanging out with friends					
Mountain climbing					
Playing ball games					
Cycling					
Boating					

Section V   Theme Extension

Part I   Reading and Discussing

Read the following short passage and discuss the questions.

A tree-climbing course was opened this school term at Northwest University in Xi'an, capital of Northwest China's Shaanxi Province. The university opened the new course to teach students special skills to help them escape from disasters, following the example set by some universities in the United States. The tree-climbing course is scheduled to have 16 classes this school term, teaching students about equipment use, field survival, climbing and descending, rope techniques and first-aid skills.

Questions:

1. Do you think this tree-climbing course important for university students? Please give three reasons at least.
2. Do you like tree climbing? Why?
3. Can you name some tree climbing skills?

Part II Scenic Spots of the World

There are some special places which have their meanings and you have to see them to feel accomplished. The purpose is to make you love the nature which is called "the biggest wonder of the world".

1. Beijing

Beijing is the capital of the People's Republic of China, the center of the nation's politics, culture and international exchanges and a modern metropolis full of vitality. It is one of the six ancient cities in China together with Xi'an, Luoyang, Kaifeng, Nanjing and Hangzhou. It had served as the capital for the dynasties such as Jin (1115 AD–1234 AD), Yuan (1279 AD–1368 AD), Ming (1368 AD–1644 AD) and Qing (1644 AD–1911 AD).

Top attractions in Beijing: Tian'anmen Square, the Forbidden City, the Temple of Heaven, the Summer Palace, the Great Wall, the Ming Tombs, Hutong, the Lama Temple, Beihai Park, Beijing Capital Museum.

2. Xi'an

Xi'an, also called Changan, is the largest city in north-west China. It had served as the nation's capital for 13 dynasties such as Western Zhou (11th century BC–771 BC), Qin (221 BC–206 BC), Western Han (206 BC–24 AD) and Tang (618 AD–907 AD) for more than 1,000 years. It is famous for historical importance.

Unit 1 Outdoor Activities

Top attractions in Xi'an: the Terra-cotta Army, Banpo Museum, Huaqing Hotspring, the City Wall, the Big Goose Pagoda, Shaanxi Provincial Museum, Xi'an Great Mosque, Forest of Stone Steles Museum.

3. Shanghai

As the largest city in China, Shanghai is located in central-eastern China, confronting the East China Sea. Shanghai is mainly sectioned into two parts: Pudong (east of the Huangpu River) and Puxi (west of the Huangpu River).

Top attractions in Shanghai: Shanghai Bund, Shanghai Jade Buddha Temple, Shanghai Yuyuan Garden, Shanghai Museum, Shanghai Xin Tian Di, Shanghai Oriental Pearl TV Tower, Shanghai Huangpu River.

Describe a town or city you would like to go with friends.
You should say:
Where would you like to go?
When would you like to go there?
Who would you like to go with?
Then explain why you would like to go there.

Section VI   Rhythm Across the Sea

Listen to the following song and sing it with your friends.

Two Weeks Holiday

I remember the last summer	in two weeks holiday
you've been my hometown	haven't you see the
for your holiday	and haven't you see the
two weeks holiday	not far from us
The sun was burning all day	you see
It can really turn your skin red	bamboo house

bamboo house
(in the forest, near by the river)
bamboo house
bamboo house
bamboo house
bamboo house
(in the forest, near by the river)
We're hand in hand in the dusk
like anyone who fall in love
in love in love in love
in love in love in love
haven't you see the
and haven't you see the
not far from us
you see
bamboo house
bamboo house
(in the forest, near by the river)

bamboo house
bamboo house
bamboo house
(in the forest, near by the river)
bamboo house
We're hand in hand in the dusk
like anyone who fall in love
in love in love in love
in love in love in love
I remember the last summer
you've been my hometown
for your holiday
two weeks holiday
The sun was burning all day
It can really turn your skin red
in two weeks holiday

Unit 1 Outdoor Activities

Section VII Pocket Poem

Appreciate the following poem and read it aloud.

Leisure
闲　暇

What is this life if, full of care, We have no time to stand and stare. No time to stand beneath the boughs, And stare as long as sheep and cows. No time to see, when woods we pass, Where squirrels hide their nuts in grass. No time to see, in broad daylight, Streams full of stars, like skies at night. No time to turn at Beauty's glance, And watch her feet, how they can dance. No time to wait till her mouth can Enrich that smile her eyes began. A poor life this is if, full of care, We have no time to stand and stare.	如果人生充满了忧虑，而无瑕 驻足赏玩，这样的人生该作何评判？ 无暇在树下止步欣赏， 像牛羊一样久久凝望。 无暇在经过树林之时， 看松鼠在草丛将坚果储藏。 无暇在明亮的白昼， 看溪中洒满星光点点，如夜空般璀璨。 无暇回应美人的顾盼， 看她双足起舞翩翩。 无暇等待她朱唇轻启， 将双眸的微笑衬托得更加灿烂。 如果人生充满了忧虑，而无瑕 驻足赏玩，这样的人生实在可怜。

Section VIII   Voice of Wisdom

You are going to listen to a famous speech. Listen carefully and try to imitate and read the passage out loud.

Fear or Faith: Which Will Be Our Master?

Speech (excerpt) at Yale Graduation presented by Tom Hanks on May 10, 2011

Fear is whispered in our ears and shouted in our faces. Faith must be fostered by the man or woman you see every day in the mirror. The former forever snaps at our heels and our synapses and delays our course. The latter can spur our boot heels to be wandering, stimulate our creativity and drive us forward.

Fear or faith? Which will be our master?

Three men found that they could no longer sleep because of their deep seeded fears, this is a story I'm telling. Their lives were in the state of stasis because of their constant worries. So they set out on a pilgrimage to find a wise man, who lived high in the mountains, so high up above the tree line, that no vegetation grew, no animals lived, not even insects could be found so high up in the mountains in that thin air. When they reached his cave, the first of the three said: "Help me, wise man, for my fear has crippled me!"

"What is your fear?" asked the wise man.

"I fear death." said the pilgrim. "I wonder when it is going to come for me."

"Ah, death." said the wise man. "Let me take away this fear, my friend. Death will not come to call until you are ready for its embrace. Know that and your fear will go away."

Well, this cumbered the pilgrim's mind and he feared death no longer. This wise man turned to the second pilgrim and said, what is your fear, my friend?"

Unit 1

Outdoor Activities

"I fear my new neighbors," said the second pilgrim. "They are strangers, who observe holy days different than mine. They have way too many kids. They play music that sounds like noise."

"Ah, strangers," said the wise man. "I will take away this fear, my friend. Return to your home, and make a cake for your new neighbors. Bring toys to their children. Join them in their songs, and learn their ways, and you will become familiar with these neighbors and your fear will go away."

The second man saw the wisdom in the simple instructions, and knew he would no longer fear the family who were his neighbors. There in the cave so high in the mountains that nothing could live, the wise man turned to the last pilgrim and asked of his fear.

"Oh, wise man, I fear spiders. when I try to sleep at night, I imagine spiders dropping from the ceiling and crawling up on my flesh and I can't rest."

"Ah, spiders," said the wise man. "No, shit, why do you think I live way up here?"

Fear will get the worst of the best of us, and peddlers of influence count on that.

Communication

Communication is an exchange of information between two or more individuals or groups. We use verbal and nonverbal cues (线索、提示) to accomplish (完成) a number of personal and relational goals. For different purposes we need communicate with one another. On various subjects we communicate our opinions, preferences and attitudes. Being good at communication is a great advantage. It can help us with presentations (展示) in classes, during job interviews, when handling arguments, and in a variety of other situations. What's more, different people prefer different ways of communication. Some like face to face communication. Others like phoning or texting messages on mobile phones. And still others prefer online communication with instant messaging software, such as e-mail, QQ, WeChat, etc.

Unit 2 Communication

Learning Objectives

In this unit you are going to:

★ learn some new words related to communication;

★ learn speaking skills — agreeing and disagreeing;

★ practice speaking around the topics given.

Section I   Words and Sentence Patterns

Part I   Words Related to Communication

Every day you may engage in a lot of communication. Now let's discover the basic elements of the communication process and learn how people exchange ideas.

Basic Elements of Communication Process

1. sender /'sendə/ 信息发送者
2. receiver /rɪ'siːvə/ 信息接收者
3. message /'mesɪdʒ/ 信息
4. channel /'tʃænəl/ 信道
5. encode /ɪn'kəʊd/ 编码
6. decode /diː'kəʊd/ 解码
7. response /rɪ'spɒns/ 反应
8. feedback /'fiːdbæk/ 反馈
9. context /'kɒntekst/ 语境
10. noise /nɔɪz/ 噪声

Part II Sentence Patterns Related to Communication

1. **A:** I love the video lesson. What about you?
   B: It was really nice, I enjoyed it and learned quite a few things.
2. **A:** How about overtime meals? Can we expense (把……记入费用账) them?
   B: Yes, submit (提交) the expense report to me.
3. **A:** Do you have any idea on the novel?
   B: That was the worst novel I've ever read. It was a complete waste of time.

Section II Conversations

Having good communication skills is important. Listen and learn the following conversations.

Conversation 1

A: What do you think of the movie? What part do you like best?
B: The scene the heroine was badly tortured by her own misdeeds was most impressive.
A: Can't agree with you more. And then I even dropped tears.
B: To tell you the truth, tears also came to my eyes.
A: It's won this year's Oscar Award.
B: It deserves it.

Conversation 2

A: Dick, have you tried the method I told you last Monday?
B: I've tried it time and time again. But it doesn't take effect.

Unit 2 Communication

A: Don't be discouraged. All we need is a little patience.
B: I know, you've expressed your attitude that day, but I've already tried my best.
A: Let's have one more try.
B: Hope we can make it.

Conversation 3

A: I want to start a trip, but I don't know where to go. What do you think about it?
B: Harbin is a good choice. You won't spend much but can enjoy yourself in the natural snowy days.
A: That's a good idea. I will go to Harbin.
B: Please share your photos on WeChat Moments. I like to appreciate all the photos about travel.
A: I will.
B: Have a good trip.

Conversation 4

A: It's been a long day. I want a drink. Would you like to go with me?
B: I don't like the idea at all. It is late, I shall go home now.
A: How do you feel about our new boss?
B: She's friendly and easy-going.
A: Well, I'm not sure about that. Perhaps, she's too bossy sometimes.
B: Yes, that's right. But except for that, I think she's nice.
A: I agree.

Conversation 5

A: Thanks for coming. Would you like to have a talk today about the way you've been communicating with some of the clients?
B: Oh, sure. What's the matter?
A: You see, you usually send e-mail to them for communication, correct?
B: Yes, that's right.

A: Well. E-mail is not always the best way of communication. You'd better choose appropriate ways in different situations.

B: OK. Thank you for your advice.

Section III Practice

I. Complete the following conversation with the phrases given.

> A. That sounds good
> B. see the places of interest
> C. make all the necessary planes, hotels, and tour reservations

A: What can I do for you?

B: My wife and I want to 1_____ in Shenzhen, Guangzhou and Zhuhai. Can you arrange a tour for us?

A: How long would you like to stay in these cities?

B: Well, three days.

A: There is a three-day package tour. You will have 3 full days in the cities.

B: 2_____. How much is the tour?

A: 2,800 yuan for each person.

B: What does it include?

A: It includes your air fare, your hotel accommodations and the meals.

B: Could we have you 3_____?

A: Yes. we could do that for you.

II. Complete the following conversation with the sentences given.

> A. I don't think so.
> B. Sounds good, I'll try.
> C. Why not?
> D. What's up?
> E. How about talking with your mother?

Unit 2 Communication

A: Hi, Lucy. You look upset. 1_____

B: Well, I love music, but my mother doesn't allow me to listen to it.

A: 2_____

B: Because she thinks listening to music is not good for my study.

A: 3_____ I also love music. It makes me relaxed and helps me study better.

B: Right. Music brings me much, too. But how can I solve my problem? Can you give me some advice?

A: Of course. 4_____

B: No, I don't often talk with her. We often argue.

A: I think communicating with each other is a better way. You can have a good talk with your mother.

B: 5_____ Thanks for your advice.

III. Match the items in Column A with the items in Column B.

A	B
1. What do you think of my new hair style?	A. Yes. I think so. That's refreshing.
2. What's your favorite way of communication?	B. It's lovely. It suits you best.
3. What do you think about painting the walls green?	C. I think it is the best one by her.
4. What's your opinion of her latest novel?	D. I don't think green is the best and only choice.
5. Do you think that hosting the party in the garden is a good idea?	E. WeChat is my favorite.

IV. Work in pairs and discuss the topic: What's your preference, face-to-face communication or electronic communication? Make a list of advantages and disadvantages of them and then give your reasons.

Ways of Communicating			
Face-to-Face Communication		Electronic Communication	
Advantages	Disadvantages	Advantages	Disadvantages
1.	1.	1.	1.
2.	2.	2.	2.
3.	3.	3.	3.
4.	4.	4.	4.
5.	5.	5.	5.

V. Tell your partner what your favorite way of communication is and when you're going to communicate in this way.

    My favorite way of communicating is _____, and I love it _____ because _____. When I communicate with _____ about _____, I prefer this way.

VI. Work in pairs and discuss the following questions.

    ★ Are you good at communicating with others?
    ★ How often do you communicate with your parents?
    ★ Is there any difference between communicating with parents and friends?

Unit 2 Communication

Section IV Speaking Skills: Expressing "Agree" or "Disagree"

There are many ways of expressing "agree" and "disagree". Read the following expressions and learn a few of them.

Agree	Disagree
I agree…	I don't agree with you.
I totally agree…	I disagree with you (entirely).
Definitely…	I don't think so.
I couldn't agree more…	I'm not so certain.
Absolutely…	I'm not sure about that.
Precisely…	I really can't agree.
I see your point…	I wouldn't go along with you there.
I see what you are getting at…	You can't be serious.
I'd go along with that view to a point…	Don't be too sure.
Sure, that's one way of looking at it…	I'm afraid I don't share your opinions.
I have to side with you on this one…	I'm afraid we don't see eye to eye on this.
I suppose so…	That's not how I see it.
I think so too…	I'm not convinced.
I'd go along with that…	I'd be inclined to disagree.
That's a good point…	That's not the way I see it.
I see exactly what you mean…	I don't feel the same.
You're right, that's a good point…	
Actually, I think you're right…	
That's true…	
Well, I agree with you here…	
You have my full agreement…	
I second that…	
OK, that's convincing…	
I take your word on it…	
You took the words right out of my mouth…	

Quiz: What are other ways of expressing "agree" or "disagree"? Choose the one that best answers the question marked A, B, C, and D.

1. Which of the following is the correct way to express her brother has similar tastes in movies? "She loves horror films."
   A. So he loves.　　B. So does he.　　C. So he does.　　D. Neither does he.

2. What is the most appropriate response to the following statement?
   "I don't like spicy food."
   A. Neither do I.　　B. So do I.　　C. So don't I.　　D. Neither do I like.

3. You say, "I love eating chocolate." Which is the correct way to express my boyfriend has similar tastes to me?
   A. Nor does my boyfriend.　　　　B. My boyfriend loves her too.
   C. And my boyfriend so does.　　　D. None of the above.

4. Someone tells you, "I couldn't swim until I was seven." Which of the following is the correct way of saying your swimming experience was similar?
   A. So could I.　　B. So couldn't I.　　C. Neither could I.　　D. Not couldn't I.

5. If someone says, "I come from China", which of the following is the correct way to express you are from China too?
   A. So do I.　　B. Nor do I.　　C. I also come.　　D. I do also.

6. Which of the following options could be a response to someone saying, "We won't be going to the party on Saturday."
   A. Neither will we.　　B. Nor will we.　　C. We won't be either.　　D. All of the above.

Section V　Theme Extension

Part I　Reading and Discussing

Read the following short passage and answer the questions.

When travelling, you may think that if you don't know the language, you can communicate

Unit 2 Communication

using gestures. However, very few gestures are universally understood and interpreted. What is perfectly acceptable in this country may be rude in other cultures.

(1) Pointing at something using the index finger. It is impolite to point with the index finger in the Middle and Far East. Use an open hand or your thumb in Indonesia.

(2) Making a "V" sign. This means "victory" in most parts of Europe when you make the sign with your palm facing away from you. But if you face your palm in, the gesture is very rude.

(3) Smiling. This facial expression is universally understood. However, cultures can provide different reasons for smiling. The Japanese may smile when they are confused or angry while in other parts of Asia people smile when they are embarrassed. People in some cultures only smile to friends. It is important not to judge people for not smiling, or for smiling at what we would consider "inappropriate" times.

(4) Waving one's hand with the palm facing outward to greet someone. In parts of Europe, waving the hand back and forth can mean "No". To wave "goodbye", raise the palm outward and wave the fingers together; but this is rude in Nigeria if the hand is too close to another person's face.

(5) Forming a circle with one's fingers to mean "OK". Although this means "OK" in the US and many other countries, there are some notable exceptions. In Brazil and Germany the gesture is obscene, while in Japan it means "money". In France, it has the additional meaning of "zero" or "worthless".

Questions:

1. According to the text, when we travel to other countries _____.
    A. many gestures are universally recognized
    B. the same gesture can have different meanings
    C. a smile always suggests friendliness
    D. we can still communicate without knowing the languages

2. Which of the following gestures should be used to point at an object in Indonesia?

   A　　　　　　B　　　　　　C　　　　　　D

3. What does the word "inappropriate" in Paragraph 4 probably mean?

A. Unsuitable.　　　　　　　　　B. Impolite.
C. Uncomfortable.　　　　　　　D. Ordinary.

4. When you talk to people from Brazil, you should remember not to _____.

   A. smile at them　　　　　　　B. make a "V" sign
   C. point at objects around you　D. make the "OK" gesture

5. The text is mainly to _____.

   A. show that gestures are universally accepted
   B. warn readers of impolite gestures
   C. show the different meanings of gestures in different countries
   D. teach readers how to understand gestures in other countries

Part II　Scenic Spots of the World

There are some special places which have their meanings and you have to see them to feel accomplished. The purpose is to make you love the nature which is called "the biggest wonder of the world".

1. Guilin

Guilin can be regarded as "Paradise on Earth" in view of its fascinating natural beauty. It is famous for its picturesque Karst landscape (喀斯特地貌), among which the Li River cruise is truly the highlight not to be missed. A leisure trip through the countryside of Yangshuo adds a different flavor. From cruising to hiking, our private Guilin tours offer clients a possibility to travel in different ways.

Top attractions in Guilin: Li River, Elephant Trunk Hill, Yangshuo Countryside, Reed Flute Cave, Rice Terraces in Longsheng, Daxu Ancient Town, Seven Star Park.

2. Chengdu

Pandas in Chengdu have a lot of fans. Their cute appearance and naive nature attract people from all over the world. Our private Chengdu tours include the top highlights of this city, which allow you to have close contact with pandas, admire the historical heritage, experience the scenic Jiuzhaigou and taste the famous Sichuan food. Travelers may linger their stay here once stepping on this wonderful place.

Top attractions in Chengdu: Panda Base, Wuhou Temple, Jinli Street, Wide and Narrow Alley, Jinsha Site Museum, Leshan Giant Buddha, Mt. Emei, Dujiangyan Irrigation System, Jiuzhaigou Scenic Area, Huanglong Scenic Area, Sichuan Cuisine Museum, Sichuan Opera.

3. Zhangjiajie

Zhangjiajie, a World Heritage Site as well as a World Geopark, is an uncanny workmanship of Mother Nature. It is a favored destination for travelers from all over the world. Following our private Zhangjiajie tours, you will see the floating mountains of Avatar (阿凡达) in reality, and have an exciting walk on the world's longest and highest glass bridge in addition to admiring the natural landscape at its best.

Top attractions in Zhangjiajie: National Forest Park, Zhangjiajie Grand Canyon, Glass Bridge, Zhangjiajie Scenic Area, Tianzi Mountain, Tianmen Mountain.

Describe a town or city you would like to go with friends.

You should say:

Where would you like to go?

When would you like to go there?

Who would you like to go with?

Then explain why you would like to go there.

Section VI　Rhythm Across the Sea

Listen to the following song and sing it with your friends.

500 Miles

If you miss the train I am on	Away from home
You will know that I am gone	Away from home
You can hear the whistle blow a hundred miles	Lord, I'm five hundred miles away from home
A hundred miles	Not a shirt on my back
A hundred miles	Not a penny to my name
A hundred miles	Lord, I can't go back home this a-way
A hundred miles	This a-way
You can hear the whistle blow a hundred miles	This a-way
	This a-way
Lord, I'm one	This a-way
Lord, I'm two	Lord, I can't go back home this a-way
Lord, I'm three	
Lord, I'm four	If you miss the train I'm on
Lord, I'm five hundred miles away from home	You will know that I am gone
Away from home	You can hear the whistle blow a hundred miles
Away from home	

Unit 2 Communication

Section VII Pocket Poem

Appreciate the following poem and read it aloud.

There Is No Frigate Like a Book
没有一艘舰船能像一本书

There is no Frigate like a Book To take us Lands away Nor any Coursers like a Page Of prancing Poetry This Traverse may the poorest take Without oppress of Toll How frugal is the Chariot That bears the Human Soul	没有一艘舰船能像一本书， 带我们遨游远方。 没有一匹骏马能像一页诗行， 如此欢跃飞扬。 即使一贫如洗， 它也可以带你走上无需路费的旅程。 这辆战车，朴素无华， 却载着人类的灵魂。

Section VIII Voice of Wisdom

You are going to listen to a famous speech. Listen carefully and try to imitate and read the passage out loud.

Best of Two Cultures

Andrea Jung, first female CEO of Avon with Chinese Heritage, speaks to students in Tsinghua University on cultural benefits in October, 2003.

As I reflect on my rapid rise to the top as one of the few women running a major global corporation, I have found myself thinking a great deal about my Chinese heritage and how enormously fortunate I am to have been given this very precious gift.

I was raised in a traditional Chinese family where achievement was not demanded, but expected. My father, born in Hong Kong, was a successful architect. My mother, born in Shanghai, was the first female chemical engineer in her graduating class at the University of Toronto in Canada. They arrived in America not speaking a word of English but through hard work, both were able to fulfill their full potential, and their success has set a wonderful example for me.

My parents were always, and continue to be today, the single biggest influence in my life. They raised my brother and me with a respect for the values and traditions of our Chinese heritage, yet also with an unwavering commitment to bring us up with all the opportunities for higher education and a desire to prepare us to adapt to American society and to succeed in this world of great change.

My brother and I were given all the opportunities of our American friends — the same schools, the same tennis lessons, the same piano teachers... but we had the wonderful advantage in my mind of a cultural heritage that we were always taught to be proud of. Mom and Dad always wanted us to be proud of

Unit 2 Communication

being Chinese — my brother and I smile today when we reminisce on growing up in our house. We grew up believing that being Chinese was the greatest advantage in life; in our house, everything important in life came from China, was invented in China, owed all to the Chinese.

We went on elementary school field trips to pulp plants, where they taught us how paper was made. "Paper was invented in China," Mom said, after we relayed the process in awe. Our favorite neighbors were Italian and invited us over for spaghetti. When we came home and raved, Dad would remind us that Marco Polo brought pasta home from China. Not Italian... Chinese... and so it went. And how wonderful they were to instill in us the sense of pride in our heritage that we have never forgotten.

When I first became a CEO, a famous American television journalist interviewed my dad and asked him if he always knew I would be successful in business. "No," he said, quite to the contrary, he worried for years that raising me to be a respectful Chinese daughter would hinder my ability to compete in a world with what he considered the aggressive, cut throat traits of typical American CEO's. In fact, he passed on a letter to me that I keep, translated from Chinese to English, in my desk drawer. The letter reads:

"Remember, there are distinctive qualities that set apart the successful Chinese... strive to excel in all you do; be a superb parent willing to curtail your own pleasure for the sake of better nurturing your children; be generous, fair, tolerant, eager to learn from other cultures while sharing your own. But beyond these attributes, remember to have an absence of arrogance and boastfulness; have unfailing courtesy, forbearance, sensitivity to others' feelings and above all, the ability to diffuse your anger and grievance, not by suppressing them but by transforming them into helpful, positive emotions. In an age and environment of pretension, you have a precious Chinese cultural heritage which we are proud to pass down to you..."

Food

"You are what you eat". What you eat becomes part of you. Your food choices each day affect your health — how you feel today, tomorrow, and in the future. A nutritious (有营养的) balanced diet is a key to good health. By making smart food choices, you can get the nutrients your body needs to stay healthy, active, and strong. Moreover, food is a major part of every culture. What you eat reveals who you are, as individuals and as a culture. Chinese cuisine (菜肴) has a number of different genres (类型), the most famous being the Eight Cuisines. Factors that establish the form of a genre include history, geography, climate, resources, cooking methods and life styles. Americans represent a wide range of backgrounds, so their eating habits differ. The variety of foods enjoyed in the US reflects the various tastes.

Unit 3 Food

Learning Objectives

In this unit you are going to:

★ learn some new words related to food;

★ learn speaking skills — asking for and expressing opinions;

★ practice speaking around the topics given.

Section I Words and Sentence Patterns

Part I Words Related to Food

Eating isn't just about satisfying hunger. Good nutrition makes a healthy life. Now let's learn some words about food.

Meat and Seafood

1. beef /biːf/	牛肉
2. pork /pɔːk/	猪肉
3. mutton /ˈmʌtən/	羊肉
4. lamb /læm/	羔羊肉
5. chicken /ˈtʃɪkɪn/	鸡肉
6. bacon /ˈbeɪkən/	咸猪肉
7. steak /steɪk/	牛排
8. sausage /ˈsɒsɪdʒ/	香肠
9. lobster /ˈlɒbstə/	龙虾
10. crab /kræb/	蟹
11. shrimp /ʃrɪmp/	小虾
12. prawn /prɔːn/	对虾，大虾
13. scallop /ˈskɒləp/	扇贝

14. oyster /ˈɔɪstə/ 牡蛎
15. jellyfish /ˈdʒelɪfɪʃ/ 海蜇
16. clam /klæm/ 蚬，蛤

Vegetables

1. pumpkin /ˈpʌmpkɪn/ 南瓜
2. sweet corn /swiːt//kɔːn/ 甜玉米
3. lettuce /ˈletɪs/ 生菜
4. cabbage /ˈkæbɪdʒ/ 卷心菜
5. carrot /ˈkærət/ 胡萝卜
6. mushroom /ˈmʌʃruːm/ 蘑菇
7. broccoli /ˈbrɒkəlɪ/ 西兰花
8. onion /ˈʌnjən/ 洋葱
9. celery /ˈselərɪ/ 芹菜
10. olive /ˈɒlɪv/ 橄榄
11. cucumber /ˈkjuːkʌmbə/ 黄瓜
12. potato /pəˈteɪtəʊ/ 马铃薯，土豆，洋芋
13. tomato /təˈmeɪtəʊ/ 番茄，西红柿
14. chilli /ˈtʃɪlɪ/ 辣椒，甜椒
15. garlic /ˈgaːlɪk/ 大蒜

Part II Sentence Patterns Related to Food

1. **A:** What main dish would you like, Tom?
   B: Well, I'd like the sirloin steak, please.
2. **A:** Would you like a dessert?
   B: What special kind of desserts do you have?
3. **A:** Does the fruit salad taste nice?
   B: Amazing! It's the best I've ever had.

Unit 3 Food

Section II Conversations

Good nutrition plays an important part in leading a healthy lifestyle. Your food choices each day affect your health. Listen and learn the following conversations.

Conversation 1

A: I think I should eat healthier.
B: I've changed my diet recently.
A: What do you eat?
B: My diet consists mainly of fruits, veggies, and chicken.
A: That's it?
B: Just about.
A: That sounds delicious and healthy.
B: You should try it. You won't be disappointed.

Conversation 2

A: I'm on a new diet.
B: What do you eat?
A: I changed from pasta to potatoes.
B: Why?
A: Pasta is processed food. Potatoes are natural.
B: Natural food has more vitamins.
A: And it's just as easy to prepare.

Conversation 3

A: What do you feel like eating this morning?
B: I usually just have cereal.

A: Breakfast is the most important meal of the day.
B: Yeah, but I don't usually have time to eat a big breakfast.
A: You can make an easy breakfast.
B: What do you make?
A: All I make is oatmeal, toast, and some orange juice.
B: That sounds pretty good.

Conversation 4

A: What'd you like today?
B: A hamburger.
A: Do you want cheese on it?
B: No cheese.
A: Can I get you something to drink?
B: Can I get a soda, please?
A: What kind do you want?
B: I'd like a Sprite.
A: Is that all?
B: That'll be all.

Conversation 5

A: Excuse me, I'd like to try some Chinese food.
B: We serve excellent Chinese food. Which style do you prefer?
A: I know nothing about Chinese food. Could you give me some suggestions?
B: It's divided into 8 big cuisines such as Cantonese food, Shandong food, Sichuan food, etc.
A: Is there any difference?
B: Yes, Cantonese food is lighter while Shandong food is heavier.
A: How about Sichuan food?

Unit 3 Food

B: Most Sichuan dishes are spicy and hot. They taste differently.
A: Oh, really. I like hot food. Thank you.
B: It's my pleasure.

Section III Practice

I. Complete the following conversation with the phrases given.

> A. sound pretty good
> B. try my best
> C. start eating healthier

A: I really need to 1_____.
B: I have to do that, too.
A: What do you eat?
B: I 2_____ to eat only fruits, veggies, and chicken.
A: Really?
B: That's it basically.
A: What about the chicken?
B: I eat baked chicken. There's not a lot of fat.
A: That does 3_____.
B: I know it does, and it really is.

II. Complete the following conversation with the sentences given.

> A. So am I.
> B. Why not have a try?
> C. How about we go eat in the cafeteria?
> D. Would you like chow mein (炒面)?

A: I'm starving.
B: 1_____

A: What's for dinner?

B: 2_____

A: What do they have?

B: Everything.

A: Well, I want Chinese food.

B: 3_____

A: 4_____

B: Trust me, the food there isn't half bad.

III. Match the items in Column A with the items in Column B.

A	B
1. How about some burgers?	A. I'd like it grilled.
2. Why aren't you eating anything else?	B. I had it yesterday.
3. I don't know what kind of sandwich I want.	C. Well, fruits and vegetables are very healthy.
4. How do you want your corn?	D. Just a peanut butter and jelly sandwich.
5. What kind of pie do you prefer?	E. I've no idea.

IV. Work in pairs and discuss the topic: What's your preference, fast food or homemade food? Make a list of advantages and disadvantages of them and then give your reasons.

Fast Food		Homemade Food	
Advantages	Disadvantages	Advantages	Disadvantages
1.	1.	1.	1.
2.	2.	2.	2.
3.	3.	3.	3.
4.	4.	4.	4.
5.	5.	5.	5.

V. Tell your partner your opinions about healthy eating.

　　The benefits of healthy eating are _____. It's easier than you think! The steps I take in improving my nutrition are _____. Here are the tips. _____. Now it's time for you to start eating healthy!

VI. Work in pairs and discuss the following questions.

★ What are your current eating habits? Are they healthy? Why?
★ Have you ever thought of eating healthier?
★ What changes can you put into your action in moving toward a healthier you?

Section IV　Speaking Skills: Asking & Expressing Opinions

How do people ask for and express opinions in English? Read the following expressions and learn a few of them.

Asking for Opinions	Expressing Opinions
1. How do you feel about …?	1. In my opinion, …
2. What do you think of …?	2. Personally, I think …
3. How do you feel about doing…?	3. To me, …
4. What's your view on the matter?	4. I believe that…
5. How do you see it?	5. As far as I'm concerned, …
6. Let's have your opinion.	6. I'm not sure how I feel about that.
7. Do you think that…?	7. I don't really have an opinion about the …
8. Do you agree that…?	8. That can't be true.
	9. But what about…?

Conduct a survey by using the following 15 questions to find out the cultural differences in the eating habits of overseas students in China.

1. What staple food do you eat in your country?
　　A. Bread.　　　　　B. Pasta.　　　　　C. Pizza.　　　　　D. Pies.
　　E. Cereals.

2. What kind of drink do you choose usually when you are in your hometown?

   A. Coffee.   B. Tea.

   C. Carbonic acid drinking (碳酸饮料).   D. Coco.

   E. Milk.

3. Have you ever eaten Chinese food before you came to China?

   A. Usually.   B. A few times.   C. Never.

4. Did you know the eating habits in China before you came here?

   A. Know a lot.   B. Know a little.   C. Have no idea.

5. How long have you been in China?

   A. Less than 3 months.   B. Less than a half of year.

   C. Less than a year.   D. 1-2 years.

   E. More than 2 years.

6. What was the reason for your first attempt at a Chinese restaurant?

   A. Tasty food.   B. Great looking.   C. Too hungry.

7. Do you like Chinese food?

   A. Yes.   B. Just fine.   C. Not really.

8. Do you often cook at home or eat at restaurants/canteens?

   A. Cook at home.   B. Eat at restaurants/canteens.

9. Which Chinese staple food do you like best?

   A. Steamed buns.   B. Rice.   C. Noodles.   D. Dumplings.

   E. Rice noodles.

10. What do you prefer when you order Chinese dishes?

    A. Flavor.   B. Nutrition.   C. Appearance.

11. What flavor would you prefer?

    A. Sweet.   B. Salty.   C. Acid.   D. Spicy.

12. How many dishes do you order when you eat at restaurants?

    A. Only 1.   B. 1 or 2.   C. 3.   D. More than 3.

13. How much do you spend usually when you eat at restaurants?

    A. 20-30 yuan.   B. 30-50 yuan.

    C. 50-100 yuan.   D. More than 100 yuan.

14. What do you think Chinese restaurants or dining halls need improve most?

    A. Flavor.   B. Dining environment.

C. Price.   D. Quality of service.
15. In what aspects is Chinese food different from the food in your country?
   A. Flavor.   B. Nutrition.   C. Appearance.

Section V   Theme Extension

Part I   Reading and Discussing

Read the following short passage and answer the questions.

If you think American cooking means opening a package and throwing the contents into the microwave, think again. On the one hand, it's true that Americans have cold cereal for breakfast, sandwiches for lunch and instant dinners. From busy homemakers to working people, many Americans enjoy the convenience of fast food that can be ready to serve in 10 minutes or less. On the other hand, many Americans recognize the value of cooking skills. Parents — especially mothers — see the importance of training their children — especially daughters. Most Americans will admit that there's nothing better than a good home — cooked meal. But with cooking, as with any other skill, good results don't happen by accident.

Probably every cook has his or her own cooking style. But there are some basic skills that most people follow. For example, baking is the main method of preparing food in America. For that reason, Americans would find it next to impossible to live without an oven. American cooks give special attention to the balance of foods, too. In planning a big meal they try to include a meat, a few vegetables, some bread or pasta and often a dessert. They also like to make sure the meal is colorful. Having several different colors of food on the plate usually makes for a healthy meal.

For those who need guidance in their cooking, or for those who have just run out of ideas, recipes (菜谱) are lifesavers. Recipes list all the ingredients (原料) for a dish (generally in the order used), the amount of each to use, and a description of how to put them together.

Questions:
1. Does the author agree that American cooking means opening a package and throwing the contents into the microwave?
2. What do Americans think is the best kind of meal?
3. Why do Americans make colorful meals?
4. What does a big meal include?
5. For what reason would Americans find it next to impossible to live without an oven?

Part II Scenic Spots of the World

There are some special places which have their meanings and you have to see them to feel accomplished. The purpose is to make you love the nature which is called "the biggest wonder of the world".

1. Harbin

Known as the "Ice City", Harbin ranks high among tourist destinations in northern China, especially in winter. The splendid St. Sofia Orthodox Church, the Centre Street and the Dragon Tower well present the city's East-meets-West architectural styles. Besides, the Ice Lantern and the Grand Snow World warmly welcome visitors for a winter tour package with its amazing ice and snow sculptures.

Top attractions in Harbin: St. Sophia Cathedral, Central Street, the Dragon Tower, Songhua River Scenic Area, Sun Island Scenic Area, Grand World of Snow, Harbin Ice and Snow Festival.

2. Lhasa

Lhasa, meaning a habitation of God in Tibet, has long been a holy destination where visitors

Unit 3 Food

look forward to going. The Potala Palace, Norbulingka Park and Tibet Museum record the great changes of the city, at the same time, exhibit traditional Tibet architectural features. The Jokhang Temple, Drepung Monastery and Sera Monastery offer unique insight into the devout pilgrims' religious lives.

Top attractions in Lhasa: Potala Palace, Namtso Lake, Jokhang Temple, Sera Monastery, Drepung Monastery, Ramoche Monastery, Ganden Monastery, Norbulingka (the Summer Palace), Chakpori Hill.

3. Dunhuang

Situated near the common boundary of Gansu, Qinghai and Xinjiang, the historical city Dunhuang is a renowned tourist destination, famous for the Mogao Caves. The landform of this area is a declining basin-plain from west to northeast, high in the north and south, and low in the middle, with Mt. Qilian in the south, Mt. Mazong in the north and desert from east to west.

Top attractions in Dunhuang: Mogao Caves, Echoing-Sand Mountain, the Crescent Lake, the Yangguan Pass, the Yumen Pass.

Discuss with your partner: Would you prefer to travel alone or with a friend?
You should say:
Do you often travel alone or with a friend?
What are the advantages of traveling alone?
What are the advantages of traveling with a friend?
Then explain which you would prefer and why.

Section VI Rhythm Across the Sea

Listen to the following song and sing it with your friends.

Yellow

Look at the stars	I drew a line
Look how they shine for you	I drew a line for you
And everything you do	Oh what a thing to do
Yeah, they were all Yellow	And it was all Yellow
I came along	Your skin
I wrote a song for you	Oh yeah, your skin and bones
And all the things you do	Turn into something beautiful
it was called Yellow	Do you know?
So then I took my turn	For you I'd bleed myself dry
Oh what a thing to have done	For you I'd bleed myself dry
And it was all Yellow	It's true
Your skin	Look how they shine for you
Oh yeah, your skin and bones	Look how they shine for you
Turn into something beautiful	Look how they shine for
Do you know? You know I love you so	Look how they shine for you
You know I love you so	Look how they shine for you
I swam across	Look how they shine
I jumped across for you	Look at the stars
Oh what a thing to do	Look how they shine for you
Cos you were all Yellow	And all the things that you do

Section VII Pocket Poem

Appreciate the following poem and read it aloud.

Tell Me
告诉我

Tell me I'm clever, Tell me I'm kind, Tell me I'm talented, Tell me I'm cute, Tell me I'm sensitive, Graceful and wise, Tell me I'm perfect — But tell me the truth.	告诉我我很聪明， 告诉我我很善良， 告诉我我很有才， 告诉我我很可爱， 告诉我我很敏锐， 优雅又智慧， 告诉我我很完美—— 但请对我说实话。

Section VIII Voice of Wisdom

You are going to listen to a famous speech. Listen carefully and try to imitate and read the passage out loud.

It Is So Painful When Mum Is Gone

By Prince Henry of Wales on the 10th anniversary of Princess Diana's death

William and I can separate life into two parts. There were those years when we were blessed with the physical presence beside us of both our mother and father.

And then there are the 10 years since our mother's death. When she was alive we completely took for granted her unrivalled love of life, laughter, fun, and folly. She was our guardian, friend, and protector. She never once allowed her unfaltering love for us to go unspoken or undemonstrated.

She will always be remembered for her amazing public work. But behind the media glare, to us, just two loving children, she was quite simply the best mother in the world. We would say that, would't we? But we miss her.

She kissed us last thing at night. Her beaming smile greeted us from school. She laughed hysterically and uncontrollably when sharing something silly she might have said or done that day. She encouraged us when we were nervous or unsure.

She, like our father, was determined to provide us with a stable and secure childhood.

To lose a parent so suddenly at such a young age — as others have experienced — is indescribably shocking and sad. It was an event which changed our lives forever, as it must have done for everyone who lost someone that night.

Unit 3 Food

But what is far more important to us now, and into the future, is that we remember our mother as she would have wished to be remembered, as she was: fun-loving, generous, down-to-earth, and entirely genuine.

We both think of her everyday.

We speak about her and laugh together at all the memories.

But put simply, she made us and so many other people happy. May this be the way that she is remembered!

Shopping

People enjoy shopping and view it as a leisure activity. Many women even view it as an entertaining way to manage high stress levels. There are various shopping venues (场所), such as shopping malls, supermarkets, convenience stores, etc. With their peculiarities, even window shopping is fun as a pastime. Nowadays, you can also shop from home for just about anything, and all you need is a computer or a mobile phone linked up to the Internet. For e-shoppers, shopping online is much easier than visiting a brick-and-mortar (实体) store. However, this easy access easily causes shopping addiction (上瘾). Shopping addiction, with an uncontrollable urge to shop, is very different from a love of shopping. It often leads to financial problems, such as overspending.

Unit 4 Shopping

Learning Objectives

In this unit you are going to:

★ learn some new words related to shopping;
★ learn speaking skills — Reception and Inquiry;
★ practice speaking around the topics given.

Section I   Words and Sentence Patterns

Part I   Words Related to Shopping

Science says: shopping really does make you happy. Now let's discover the words and expressions about shopping.

Shopping

1. shopping centre /'ʃɒpɪŋ//'sentə/   商业中心区
2. department store /dɪ'pɑːtmənt//stɔː/   百货商店
3. supermarket /'suːpəˌmɑːkɪt/   超市
4. children's goods store /'tʃɪldrən s//gʊdz//stɔː/ 儿童用品商店
5. antique store /æn'tiːk//stɔː/   古玩店
6. second-hand store /'sekənd'hænd//stɔː/   旧货店
7. show window /ʃəʊ//'wɪndəʊ/   橱窗
8. show case /ʃəʊ//keɪs/   玻璃柜台
9. cash desk /kæʃ//desk/   收银台
10. price tag /praɪs//tæg/   价签
11. special offer /'speʃəl//'ɒfə/   特价
12. on sale /ɒn//seɪl/   打折
13. buy one and get one for free   买一赠一
14. online shopping /'ɒn'laɪn//'ʃɒpɪŋ/   网购

Part II Sentence Patterns Related to Shopping

1. **A:** Will the book arrive in a week?
   B: Yes. How many do you want?
2. **A:** Do you have the Oxford English Dictionary?
   B: I'm sorry. It's out of stock.
3. **A:** Are these books on sale?
   B: There's a 20% discount for members only.

Section II Conversations

People who like to spend their free time shopping are often frowned upon (不赞成). However, multiple studies have shown the various health benefits of shopping and "retail therapy (购物疗法)". Listen and learn the following conversations.

Conversation 1

A: Can I help you find something?
B: I'd like to buy a new mobile phone.
A: Is there one in particular that you like?
B: I am looking at this Huawei P10.
A: Ah yes, that is a great phone.
B: What's so great about it?
A: It's affordable. And its Leica front camera offers amazing self portraits.
B: Wow! You're right! It's great. I'll take it.

Unit 4 Shopping

Conversation 2

A: Can you help me find a coffee pot?
B: Are you looking for a small, medium, or large one?
A: I prefer a big one.
B: Is this one OK?
A: Yes, it's the right size, but it weighs a little bit too heavy.
B: Well, what do you think of the medium one?
A: It's light enough. My family's going to love this one. I'll take it.

Conversation 3

A: Hello. Do you have anything for a little boy?
B: Well, we have the latest Lego sets.
A: That's a great idea. Let me have a look.
B: Here's one — Lego batman. It's really cool!
A: How lovely! How much is it?
B: It's only $23.99.
A: Too much fun in one little box! Let me have one.

Conversation 4

A: I need to buy a new laptop.
B: Where are you going to find one?
A: I have no idea.
B: Do you want to know where I bought mine?
A: Where'd you get it from?
B: I got it from an online store.
A: Does it work well?
B: Yes. The quality is fantastic.

Conversation 5

A: Thank you for purchasing your new air conditioner with us.
B: Do you have installation service?
A: Yes. When do you want it installed?
B: I need it installed tomorrow. Is it possible?
A: What time exactly?
B: How about 10:00 tomorrow morning?
A: We can do that at that time.
B: That's great! Thank you very much.

Section III Practice

I. Complete the following conversation with the phrases given.

> A. I like
> B. in the fitting room
> C. looks great though

A: I'm going to go try these on 1_____.
B: What did you find?
A: A pair of shoes and a silk dress.
B: Go try them on.
A: Alright, how do I look?
B: You look great in that dress.
A: What do you think of the shoes?
B: They are not the type 2_____.
A: I really don't think they look good.
B: That dress 3_____.
A: I'm just going to buy the dress.
B: That would be wise.

Unit 4 Shopping

II. Complete the following conversation with the sentences given.

A. What about you?
B. That would be great.
C. Have you found anything that you like?
D. Where did you get them?

A: What are you going to buy?
B: I need some new clothes. 1_____
A: I'm trying to find some clothes myself.
B: 2_____
A: I got a new pair of pants.
B: Those are cute. 3_____
A: I bought them at JCPennies.
B: I really like those.
A: I'll show you where to get them.
B: 4_____

III. Match the items in Column A with the items in Column B.

A	B
1. I'm searching for an old camera.	A. Aisle A is where you'll find all the produce.
2. Hi, do you know a place that sells cheap cashmere sweaters?	B. You came to the right place. Any particular decade?
3. Where can I find the produce?	C. I'm very sorry. The sale ended yesterday.
4. Is this dress on sale?	D. Little girls just go wild over Barbie dolls.
5. Can you help me pick out a gift for my niece?	E. An outlet carries what you want.

VI. Work in pairs and discuss the topic: What's your preference, shopping online or shopping in brick-and-mortar stores? Make a list of advantages and disadvantages of them and then give your reasons.

Shopping Online		Shopping in Stores	
Advantages	Disadvantages	Advantages	Disadvantages
1.	1.	1.	1.
2.	2.	2.	2.
3.	3.	3.	3.
4.	4.	4.	4.
5.	5.	5.	5.

V. Tell your partner what your favorite way of shopping is and why you love it best of all.

My favorite way of shopping is _____, and I love it because _____, _____, and _____. I like this way best.

VI. Work in pairs and discuss the following questions.

★ Shopping is a pleasurable pastime or form of entertainment. Do you agree? Why or why not?
★ Where do you like to go shopping?
★ Do you think shopping can really make you happy?

Section IV Speaking Skills: Reception and Inquiry

How do people express reception and inquiry in English? Read the following expressions and learn a few of them.

Reception	Inquiry
What can I do for you?	What is the price of this?
Can I help you?	How much do I have to pay you?
Are you being served?	How much does this cost?
Is there anybody waiting on you?	How much do you charge for it?
Is there one in particular that you like?	Can I have a discount?
Do you find anything you like?	Do you have a discount?

Unit 4 Shopping

Self-assessment: Are you a victim of shopping addiction? Here is a test you can do. Discuss the following questions with your partner.

If you are still trying to figure out whether or not you are a shopaholic (购物狂), shopaholics anonymously (匿名的) suggest that you ask yourself the following questions. If you answer "yes" to many of these questions, you may have an addiction. The questions are:

- Do you shop when you feel angry or disappointed?
- Has overspending created problems in your life?
- Do you have conflicts with your loved ones about your need to shop?
- While shopping, do you feel euphoric (欣快的) rushes or anxiety?
- After shopping, do you feel like you have just finished doing something wild or dangerous?
- After shopping, do you ever feel guilty or embarrassed about what you have done?
- Do you frequently buy things that you never end up using or wearing?
- Do you think about money almost all the time?

Section V   Theme Extension

Part I   Reading and Discussing

Read the following short passage and discuss the questions.

Shopping is not as simple as you may think! There are all sorts of tricks at play each time we reach out for that particular brand of product on the shelf.

Coloring for example varies according to what the producers are trying to sell. Health foods are packaged in greens, yellows or browns because we think of these as healthy colors. Ice cream packers are often blue and expensive goods like chocolates are gold or silver.

When some kind of pain killer was brought out recently researchers found that the colors turned the customers off because they made the product look weak

and ineffective. Eventually it came on the market in a dark blue and white package — blue because we think of it as safe and white as calm.

The size of a product can attract a shopper. But quite often a bottle doesn't contain as much as it appears to.

It is believed that the better-known companies spend on average 70 per cent of the total cost of the product itself on packaging!

The most successful producers know that it's not enough to have a good product. The founder of Pears soap who for 25 years has used pretty little girls to promote their goods came to the conclusion: "Any fool can make soap but it takes a genius to sell it."

Questions:

1. According to the passage, why is shopping not so simple as you may think?
2. According to the passage, what can trick a shopper into buying a product?
3. What is the meaning of the phrase "the color turned the customers off"(in Para 3)?
4. According to the passage, what else can attract a shopper in addition to coloring?
5. What does the conclusion mean that "Any fool can make soap but it takes a genius to sell it." ?

Part II　　Scenic Spots of the World

There are some special places which have their meanings and you have to see them to feel accomplished. The purpose is to make you love the nature which is called "the biggest wonder of the world".

1. Hangzhou

Hangzhou is the capital of Zhejiang Province and the local political, economic and cultural center. As the southern terminus of the Grand Canal, the city is located on the lower reaches of the Qiantang River in southeast China, a superior position on the Yangtze Delta and only 112 miles (180 km) from Shanghai.

Top attractions in Hangzhou: West Lake, Grand Canal,

Unit 4 Shopping

Wuzhen Water Town, Thousand Islets Lake, Xitang Water Town, Temple of Soul's Retreat.

2. Nanjing

Lying on the south bank of the Yangtze River, Nanjing, the capital of Jiangsu Province, is one of the most delightful destinations in China. Known as the capital city of six or ten dynasties in ancient Chinese history, it has a brilliant cultural heritage.

Top attractions in Nanjing: Confucius Temple (Fuzimiao), Xiaoling Mausoleum of the Ming Dynasty, Dr. Sun Yat-sen's Mausoleum, Qinhuai River, Nanjing City Wall, Presidential Palace, Purple Mountain, Purple Mountain Observatory.

3. Dali

Located in the northwest of the Yunnan Province, 300 kilo-meters (186 miles) northwest of Kunming, Dali City is the economic and cultural center of the Dali Bai Autonomous Prefecture. The area is surrounded by mountains on the east, west, and south, and has the Erhai Lake in its center. Here you will find 25 ethnic minorities, which have created a unique cultural heritage amidst the area's picturesque surroundings.

Top attractions in Dali: Dali Ancient City, Erhai Lake, Cangshan Mountain, Three Pagodas, Yan's Compound, Butterfly Spring, Dali Bai Autonomous Prefecture Museum, Dali Municipal Museum, Tie-dyeing.

Discuss with your partner a trip you've ever had.
You should say:
1. Where did you go? Who did you go with?
2. What did you see there? What did you do there?
3. What was the most impressive for you?
Then explain why you would like to share it with your partner.

Section VI Rhythm Across the Sea

Listen to the following song and sing it with your friends.

Photograph

Loving can hurt
Loving can hurt sometimes
But it's the only thing that I've known
When it gets hard
You know it can get hard sometimes
It is the only thing that makes us feel alive
We keep this love in a photograph
We made these memories for ourselves
Where our eyes are never closing
Our hearts were never broken
And times forever frozen still
So you can keep me inside the pocket of your ripped jeans
Holding me close until our eyes meet
You won't ever be alone
Wait for me to come home

Loving can heal
Loving can mend your soul
And it's the only thing that I've known
I swear it will get easier
Remember that with every piece of ya
And it's the only thing to take with us when we die
We keep this love in a photograph
We made these memories for ourselves
Where our eyes are never closing
Our hearts were never broken
And times forever frozen still

So you can keep me inside the pocket of your ripped jeans
Holding me close until our eyes meet
You won't ever be alone
And if you hurt me that's okay baby
Only words bleed
Inside these pages you just hold me
And I will never let you go
Wait for me to come home
Wait for me to come home
Wait for me to come home
Wait for me to come home
And you could fit me inside the necklace you got
When you were sixteen
Next to your heart right where I should be
Keep it deep within your soul
And if you hurt me
But that's okay baby
Only words bleed
Inside these pages you just hold me
And I won't ever let you go

When I'm away
I will remember how you kissed me
Under the lamppost back on 6th street
Hearing you whisper through the phone
Wait for me to come home

Unit 4 Shopping

Section VII   Pocket Poem

Appreciate the following poem and read it aloud.

Life... What is it?
生命……是什么？

See it in the colors of autumn, A gentle snowfall in winter, A sudden shower in spring, The radiance of a summer day. Behold it in the laughter Of the young and the old. Know of it in a surge of hope, The blessings that are bountiful. What is life? It is joy, awareness, And the music within.	看呀，生命是绚烂的秋色， 轻盈的冬雪， 春天的骤雨， 夏日的暖阳。 瞧呀，生命是童叟的欢笑。 体味生命， 怀着满心的希望， 带着丰盛的祝福。 生命是什么？ 是喜乐，是领悟， 是心灵深处的音乐。

Section VIII　Voice of Wisdom

You are going to listen to a famous speech. Listen carefully and try to imitate and read the passage out loud.

Looking for a Job? Highlight Your Ability, Not Your Experience.

You know who I'm envious of? People who work in a job that has to do with their college major.

Journalists who studied journalism, engineers who studied engineering. The truth is, these folks are no longer the rule, but the exception. A 2010 study found that only a quarter of college graduates work in a field that relates to their degree.

I graduated with not one but two degrees in biology. To my parents' dismay, I am neither a doctor nor a scientist.

Years of studying DNA replication and photosynthesis did little to prepare me for a career in technology. I had to teach myself everything from sales, marketing, strategy, even a little programming, on my own.

I had never held the title of Product Manager before I sent my resume to Etsy. I had already been turned down by Google and several other firms and was getting frustrated. The company had recently gone public, so as part of my job application, I read the IPO filings from cover to cover and built a website from scratch which included my analysis of the business and four ideas for new features. It turned out the team was actively working on two of those ideas and had seriously considered a third. I got the job.

We all know people who were ignored or overlooked at first but went on to prove their critics wrong. My favorite story? Brian Acton, an engineering manager who was rejected by both Twitter and Facebook before cofounding WhatsApp, the mobile messaging platform that would sell for 19 billion dollars.

The hiring systems we built in the 20th century are failing us and causing us to miss out on people with incredible potential. The

Unit 4 Shopping

advances in robotics and machine learning are transforming the way we work, automating routine tasks in many occupations while augmenting and amplifying human labor in others. At this rate, we should all be expecting to do jobs we've never done before for the rest of our careers. So what are the tools and strategies we need to identify tomorrow's high performers? In search for answers, I've consulted with leaders across many sectors, read dozens of reports and research papers and conducted some of my own talent experiments. My quest is far from over, but here are three ideas to take forward.

One: expand your search. If we only look for talent in the same places we always do — gifted child programs, Ivy League schools, prestigious organizations — we're going to get the same results we always have. Baseball was transformed when the cash-strapped Oakland Athletics started recruiting players who didn't score highly on traditionally valued metrics, like runs batted in, but who had the ability to help the team score points and win games. This idea is taking hold outside of sports. The head of Design and Research at Pinterest told me that they've built one of the most diverse and high-performing teams in Silicon Valley because they believe that no one type of person holds a monopoly on talent. They've worked hard to look beyond major tech hubs and focus on designers' portfolios, not their pedigrees.

Two: hire for performance. Inspired by my own job experience, I cofounded a hiring platform called Headlight, which gives candidates an opportunity to shine. Just as teams have tryouts and plays have auditions, candidates should be asked to demonstrate their skills before they're hired. Our clients are benefiting from 85 years of employment research, which shows that work samples are one of the best predictors of success on the job. If you're hiring a data analyst, give them a spreadsheet of historical data and ask them for their key insights. If you're hiring a marketing manager, have them plan a launch campaign for a new product. And if you're a candidate, don't wait for an employer to ask. Seek out ways to showcase your unique skills and abilities outside of just the standard resume and cover letter.

Three: get the bigger picture. I've heard about recruiters who are quick to label a candidate a job-hopper based on a single short stint on their resume; read about professors who are more likely to ignore identical messages from students because their names are black or Asian instead of white.

I was almost put on a special needs track as a child. A month into kindergarten, my teacher wrote a page-long memo noting that I was impulsive, had a short attention span, and despite my wonderful curiosity, I was exhausting to work with.

The principal asked my parents into a meeting, asked my mother if there had been  complications at birth and suggested I meet with a school psychologist. My father saw what was happening and quickly explained our family situation. As recent immigrants, we lived in the attic of a home that cared for adults with mental disabilities. My parents worked nights to make ends meet, and I had little opportunity to spend time with kids my own age. Is it really a surprise that an understimulated five-year-old boy might be a little excited in a kindergarten classroom after an entire summer by himself?

Until we get a holistic view of someone, our judgment of them will always be flawed. Let's stop equating experience with ability, credentials with competence. Let's stop settling for the safe, familiar choice and leave the door open for someone who could be amazing. We need employers to let go of outdated hiring practices and embrace new ways of identifying and cultivating talent, and candidates can help by learning to tell their story in powerful and compelling ways. We could live in a world where people are seen for what they're truly capable of and have the opportunity to realize their full potential. So let's go out and build it.

Thank you.

Transportation

  Transportation is the movement of human and goods from one location to another. In modern society transportation is facilitated by road, air, rail, and waterways. Passenger travel mainly occurs by automobile for shorter distances, and airplane or railroad for longer distances. And most cargoes travel by railroad, truck, pipeline, or boat. Each mode of transportation has its own advantages and disadvantages. A particular mode is chosen for a trip on the basis of cost, capability, and route.

Learning Objectives

In this unit you are going to:
- ★ learn some new words related to transportation;
- ★ learn speaking skills — expressing preferences;
- ★ practice speaking around the topics given.

Section I   Words and Sentence Patterns

Part I   Words Related to Transportation

Transportation plays a significant role in our daily life. Now let's discover the words and expressions about transportation.

Transportation

1. mode of transportation /məʊd//əv//ˌtrænspɔːˈteɪʃən/   交通/运输方式
2. road transportation /rəʊd//ˌtrænspɔːˈteɪʃən/   公路交通
3. automobile /ˈɔːtəməbiːl/   汽车
4. bus /bʌs/   公交车
5. taxi/cab /ˈtæksɪ//kæb/   出租车
6. tram /træm/   电车
7. subway /ˈsʌbweɪ/   地铁
8. truck /trʌk/   卡车
9. van /væn/   厢式货车
10. rail transportation /reɪl//ˌtrænspɔːˈteɪʃən/   铁路交通
11. CRH (China Railway High-speed)   中国铁路高速列车
12. D-series High-speed Train   动车组列车
13. Z-series Train   直达列车
14. waterway transportation /ˈwɔːtəweɪ//ˌtrænspɔːˈteɪʃən/   水路交通
15. passenger ship /ˈpæsɪndʒə//ʃɪp/   客船
16. freighter /ˈfreɪtə/   货船
17. yacht /jɒt/   游艇
18. airplane/aero plane /ˈeərəpleɪn;ˈeərəʊ//pleɪn/   飞机
19. helicopter /ˈhelɪkɒptə/   直升机
20. pipeline transportation /ˈpaɪplaɪn//ˌtrænspɔːˈteɪʃən/   管道交通

Unit 5 Transportation

| Part II | Sentence Patterns Related to Transportation |

1. **A:** I prefer public transport. What is the public transportation like near your apartment?
   B: There's a bus stop a few blocks away.
2. **A:** Is the bus ride long?
   B: It takes 45 minutes to an hour.
3. **A:** Is there access to public transportation near the library?
   B: Yes, there's a subway station within walking distance.

Section II   Conversations

Different people have different preferences to modes of transportation. Listen and learn the following conversations.

Conversation 1

A: So, how should we get to our university? What's your preference?
B: I'd prefer to take the bus.
A: I hate the heavy traffic at the moment! During rush hours buses are only crawling.
B: Then we could take the subway.
A: OK. We'd better hurry up, or we'll be late.
B: Don't worry. Just take your time.

Conversation 2

A: I think I'll have to consider changing from my car to the public transport.

B: The public system in our city is pretty good. It offers many options to choose from.

A: I know. I feel bad about how much my car is adding to the pollution problem in this city.

B: What would you prefer? Taking the bus or the subway?

A: The subway. Congestion is an issue and subway travel is much quicker than other modes of transportation.

B: That's true!

Conversation 3

A: Good morning. What can I do for you?

B: Yes, I'd like to book a ticket to Hong Kong next week.

A: When do you want to fly?

B: Monday, December 15.

A: We have CA101 on Monday. It leaves at 8:06 Monday morning.

B: OK. I'll take the 8:06 flight.

A: Would you like to go first class or coach class?

B: I'd prefer first class.

Conversation 4

A: Hello! I need to get to the National Center for the Performing Arts. I would prefer to take the bus, but I don't know which bus to catch.

B: Where exactly are you coming from?

A: I'm coming from Wangfujing area.

B: You can catch the 99.

A: Would you like to tell me which direction it should be going?

B: Please make sure to catch it going west.

Unit 5 Transportation

A: Where do I get off?
B: At Tian'anmen West.
A: Thanks!
B: You're welcome.

Conversation 5

A: How can I get to the airport?
B: You have quite a few options. Which means of transport would you prefer?
A: I prefer a taxi. Where can I get a taxi?
B: Just outside the hotel. WeChat or Alipay users can book a taxi with the App.
A: How much is it going to cost?
B: The city taxis have a meter so you pay by the mile.
A: Is the tip included in the fare?
B: No. How much you tip is up to you.
A: Does the taxi take credit cards?
B: No. You can pay by cash, WeChat or Alipay.
A: Thanks for the help.
B: Don't mention it.

Section III Practice

I. Complete the following conversation with the phrases given.

> A. our flight was delayed
> B. supposed to arrive
> C. most time of the flight

A: Is everything fine?
B: Yes, everything is OK.
A: Why did it take so long? I thought your flight was 1_____ 1 hour ago!

B: Was it announced that 2_____?

A: I haven't heard it. What happened?

B: There was some bad turbulence for 3_____.

A: That's normal, isn't it?

B: Yes.

II. Complete the following conversation with the sentences given.

> A. I'm not sure.
> B. What would you like to know?
> C. It's not hard to get it.
> D. Yes, they do.

A: Could you tell me more about the apartment?

B: Of course. 1_____

A: Do buses or subways run by the apartment?

B: 2_____

A: Where are the bus stop and the subway station?

B: 3_____

A: I can check online. 4_____

B: Good luck!

A: Thank you!

III. Match the items in Column A with the items in Column B.

A	B
1. Which route does the bus travel by?	A. Your seat is right here. Seat 10A.
2. Would you mind trading your seat with me?	B. Not at all.
3. Where are the safety belts?	C. I don't know, but I'm pretty sure you can find out that stuff online.
4. Can you show me the way to my seat?	D. On the side of the seat.
5. Do you know anything about the buses that stop here?	E. I wish I could help you, but I know nothing about the bus system.

Unit 5
Transportation

IV. Work in pairs and compare different modes of cargo transport: Make a list of advantages and disadvantages of them and fill in the table.

Modes of Transportation	Cost	Convenience	Delivery Speed	Safety	Risk of Damage
✈					
🚄					
🚚					
🚢					

V. Tell your partner what your favorite mode of transportation is for a long distance and why you love it best of all.

My favorite mode of transportation is _____, and I love it because _____, _____, and _____ . That's why I like it best.

VI. Work in pairs and describe the mode of transportation in the following picture.
You should say:
★ what it is.
★ how often it is used.
★ why it is popular in Venice.
★ what are its advantages and disadvantages.

Section IV Speaking Skills: Expressing Preferences

How do people talk about what they want in English? How do they express their personal preference? Read the following expressions and learn a few of them.

Preferences	
I prefer subway travel.	Do you prefer CRH or Z-series trains?
I prefer booking a taxi.	
I would prefer riding a Mobike.	Would you prefer the 10:00 flight?
I would prefer to travel by air.	
She would rather take the train.	Would you rather book the coach class?
She would rather walk than take the bus.	

Conduct a survey by using the following form to find out which modes of transportation your classmates prefer and why.

Modes of Transportation	Love	Like	OK	Dislike	Hate
airplane					
train					
ship					
subway					
bus					
car					
bike					
foot					

Unit 5 Transportation

Section V Theme Extension

Part I Reading and Discussing

Read the following short passage and discuss the questions.

If you live in a major city that offers the option of traveling by subway, you're in luck. Although you may at first miss the freedom of traveling in your automobile, you'll soon discover that subway transit can be far superior. Traveling by subway is inexpensive, convenient, safe and environmentally friendly.

If you think it's cheaper to drive your car to work rather than take the subway, you're probably mistaken. When you take into account car repairs, fuel, loan payments, parking fees, insurance, taxes and licensing, you'll be surprised at how much you spend. AAA reports that the average automobile driver spent over $9,000 in 2009 (over $24 per day), and that's before car loans were considered. On the other hand, subway transportation is economical. Many subway systems offer an unlimited monthly pass for a reasonable rate (Boston's MBTA offers such a pass for only $59 in 2010). Some employees, such as federal workers in Washington D.C., can be reimbursed(偿还) for their subway transit costs.

In cities where congestion(拥堵) is an issue, subway travel is much quicker than other modes of transportation. In this respect, subways even have the edge over public buses, as they can avoid any street congestion by literally going underneath it. Subway travel also has other conveniences. For instance, you won't have to worry about auto maintenance or buses breaking down.

Although subway accidents make for sensational(耸人听闻的) news stories, they are actually quite safe. According to publictransportation.org, ditching(放弃) the car and taking public transit saves 200,000 deaths every year. If you are worried about subways becoming potential terror targets, many subway systems now feature state-of-the-art cameras and chemical sensors for your safety.

Subway travel is extremely green. Not only is it more environmentally friendly than automobile travel, it is also has the advantage over public bus systems, as subways do not emit harmful exhaust fumes into the air.

Questions:

1. According to the passage, what are the benefits of subway travel?
2. According to the passage, is it cheaper to drive your car to work rather than take the subway?
3. Why does the author say subways even have the edge over public buses?
4. According to the passage, what do subway systems do to guarantee safety?
5. Why does the author say subway travel is extremely green? Do you agree? Why or why not?

Part II Scenic Spots of the World

There are some special places which have their meanings and you have to see them to feel accomplished. The purpose is to make you love the nature which is called "the biggest wonder of the world".

1. Singapore

With its blend of Asian and European cultures, Singapore is one of the great cities of the world. It boasts one of the world's busiest ports. Graceful colonial buildings co-exist alongside centuries-old street markets and modern high-rises. Singapore's public transport system is one of the best in the world, so you should have no problem finding your way around like a local. Travelers can't help but be fascinated by this multi-cultural city.

Top attractions in Singapore: Marina Bay Sands, Singapore Flyer, Buddha Tooth Relic Temple, Night Safari, Singapore Botanic Gardens, Gardens by the Bay, Raffles Hotel, Clarke Quay, Resorts World Sentosa, Orchard Road.

Unit 5

Transportation

2. Kyoto

Kyoto served as Japan's capital and the emperor's residence from 794 until 1868. It is one of the country's ten largest cities with a population of 1.5 million people and a modern face. Countless temples, shrines and other historically priceless structures survive in the city today.

Top attractions in Kyoto: Nijo Castle (Nijojo), Sento Imperial Palace, Tofukuji Temple, Nanzenji Temple, Kyoto National Museum, Higashiyama District, Tenryuji Temple.

3. Chiang Mai

Chiang Mai is a land of misty mountains and colorful hill tribes, a playground for seasoned travelers, a paradise for shoppers and a delight for adventurers. Located 700 km (435 miles) north of Bangkok in a verdant valley on the banks of the Ping River, Chiang Mai was founded in 1296 as the capital of the ancient Lanna Kingdom. Today it is a place where past and the present seamlessly merge with modern buildings standing side by side with venerable temples.

Top attractions in Chiang Mai: Doi Suthep; Old City Temples; Chiang Mai Night Safari; Wiang Kum Kam, the Underground Ancient City; Elephant Jungle Sanctuary Chiang Mai; Doi Inthanon National Park; Doi Pui Tribal Village and National Park; Bo Sang Handicraft Village; Lanna Folklife Museum.

Have a discussion with your partner.

You should say:

1. What are the advantages of package tours?
2. What are the advantages of DIY tours?
3. Which do you prefer? Why?

Section VI Rhythm Across the Sea

Listen to the following song and sing it with your friends.

Yesterday

Yesterday, all my troubles seemed so far away. Now it looks as though they're here to stay. Oh, I believe in yesterday. Suddenly, I'm not half the man I used to be. There's a shadow hanging over me. Oh, yesterday came suddenly. Why she had to go I don't know, she wouldn't say. I said something wrong, now I long for yesterday.	Yesterday, love was such an easy game to play. Now I need a place to hide away. Oh, I believe in yesterday. Why she had to go I don't know, she wouldn't say. I said something wrong, now I long for yesterday. Yesterday, love was such an easy game to play. Now I need a place to hide away. Oh, I believe in yesterday.

Unit 5 Transportation

Section VII Pocket Poem

Appreciate the following poem and read it aloud.

Never Give Up
永不放弃

Never give up, Never lose hope. Always have faith, It allows you to cope. Trying times will pass, As they always do. Just have patience, Your dreams will come true. So put on a smile, You'll live through your pain. Know it will pass, And strength you will gain. 	永不放弃, 永不心灰意冷。 永存信念, 它会使你应付自如。 难挨的时光终将过去, 一如既往。 只要有耐心, 梦想就会成真。 露出微笑, 你会走出痛苦。 相信苦难定会过去, 你将重获力量。 

Section VIII Voice of Wisdom

You are going to listen to a famous speech. Listen carefully and try to imitate and read the passage out loud.

The 3A's of Awesome

Addressed by Neil Pasricha, the founder of the website: 1000awesomethings.com.

I said I wanted to do three things with you today. I said I wanted to tell you the awesome story, I wanted to share with you the three A's of awesome (了不起的), and I wanted to leave you with a closing thought. So let's talk about those three A's.

Over the last few years, I haven't had that much time to really think. But lately I have had the opportunity to take a step back and ask myself: "What is it over the last few years that helped me grow my website, but also grow myself?" And I've summarized those things, for me personally, as three A's. They are Attitude(态度), Awareness(感知) and Authenticity(真实). I'd love to just talk about each one briefly.

So Attitude: Look, we're all going to get lumps, and we're all going to get bumps. None of us can predict the future, but we do know one thing about it and that's that it ain't gonna go according to plan. We will all have high highs and big days and proud moments of smiles on graduation stages, father-daughter dances at weddings and healthy babies screeching in the delivery room, but between those high highs, we may also have some lumps and some bumps too. It's sad, and it's not pleasant to talk about, but your husband might leave you, your girlfriend could cheat, your headaches might be more serious than you thought, or your dog could get hit by a car on the street. It's not a happy thought, but your kids could get mixed up in gangs or bad scenes. Your mom could get cancer, your dad could get mean. And there are times in life when you will be tossed in the well, too, with twists in your stomach and

Unit 5
Transportation

with holes in your heart, and when that bad news washes over you, and when that pain sponges and soaks in, I just really hope you feel like you've always got two choices. One, you can swirl and twirl and gloom and doom forever, or two, you can grieve and then face the future with newly sober eyes. Having a great attitude is about choosing option number two, and choosing, no matter how difficult it is, no matter what pain hits you, choosing to move forward and move on and take baby steps into the future.

I wanted to share with you the three A's of awesome, and I wanted to leave you with a closing. The second "A" is Awareness. I love hanging out with three-year-olds. I love the way that they see the world, because they're seeing the world for the first time. I love the way that they can stare at a bug crossing the sidewalk. I love the way that they'll stare  slack-jawed at their first baseball game with wide eyes and a mitt on their hand, soaking in the crack of the bat and the crunch of the peanuts and the smell of the hot dogs. I love the way that they'll spend hours picking dandelions in the backyard and putting them into a nice centerpiece for Thanksgiving dinner. I love the way that they see the world, because they're seeing the world for the first time. Having a sense of awareness is just about embracing your inner three-year-old, because you all used to be three-year-olds. That three-year-old boy is still part of you. That three-yer-old girl is still part of you. They're in there. And being aware is just about remembering that you saw everything you've seen for the first time once, too. So there was a time when it was your first time ever hitting a string of green lights on the way home from work. There was the first time you walked by the open door of a bakery and smelt the bakery air, or the first time you pulled a 20-dollar bill out of your old jacket pocket and said, " Found money."

 The last "A" is Authenticity. And for this one, I want to tell you a quick story. Let's go all the way back to 1932 when, on a peanut farm in Georgia, a little baby boy named Roosevelt Grier was born. Roosevelt Grier, or Rosey Grier, as people used to call him, grew up and grew into a 300-pound, six-foot five linebacker in the NFL. He's number 76 in the picture. Here he is pictured with the "fearsome foursome". These were four guys on the L.A. Rams in the 1960s you did not want to go up against. They were tough football players doing what they love, which was crushing skulls and separating shoulders on the football field. But Rosey Grier

also had another passion. In his deeply authentic self, he also loved needlepoint. He loved knitting. He said that it calmed him down, it relaxed him, it took away his fear of flying and helped him meet chicks. That's what he said. I mean, he loved it so much that, after he retired from the NFL, he started joining clubs. And he even put out a book called "Rosey Grier's Needlepoint for Men". It's a great cover. If you notice, he's actually needle pointing his own face.

And so what I love about this story is that Rosey Grier is just such an authentic person. And that's what authenticity is all about. It's just about being you and being cool with that. And I think when you're authentic, you end up following your heart, and you put yourself in places and situations and in conversations that you love and that you enjoy. You meet people that you like talking to. You go places you've dreamt about. And you end up following your heart and feeling very fulfilled.

So those are the three A's.

Unit 6 Travel

  Travel is the movement of people between distant locations. Travel can be done by foot, bicycle, automobile, train, boat, bus, airplane, or other means, with or without luggage, and can be one way or round trip. Reasons for traveling include recreation, tourism or vacationing, research travel, visiting people, volunteer travel for charity, migration to begin life somewhere else, religious tours, business travel, trade, commuting, and other reasons, such as to get health care or fleeing war or for the enjoyment of traveling.

Learning Objectives

In this unit you are going to:
★ learn some new words related to travel;
★ learn speaking skills — making comparisons;
★ practice speaking around the topics given.

Section I　Words and Sentence Patterns

Part I　Words Related to Travel

You may travel a lot in your life. Do you know how to talk about travel in English? Now let's learn some key words related to travel.

Travel and Hotels

1. package tour /'pækɪdʒ//tʊə/　　包价旅游
2. accommodation /ə,kɒmə'deɪʃn/　　住处
3. car rental /kɑː//'rentəl/　　租车
4. cruise line /kruːz//laɪn/　　邮轮
5. reservation /,rezə'veɪʃən/　　预定
6. travel agent /'trævəl//'eɪdʒənt/　　旅行代理人
7. travel brochure /'trævəl//'brəʊʃə/　　旅游产品宣传页
8. travel guidebook /'trævəl/ 'gaɪdbʊk/　　旅行指南
9. passport /'pɑːspɔːt/　　护照
10. visa /'viːzə/　　签证
11. vaccination [,væksɪ'neɪʃən]　　接种
12. resort /rɪ'zɔːt/　　度假村
13. B&B (bed and breakfast)　　仅提供住处和早餐的民宿
14. inn /ɪn/　　小旅馆
15. youth hostel /juːθ//'hɒstəl/　　青年旅社
16. reception /rɪ'sepʃən/　　酒店接待处
17. double room /'dʌbəl//ruːm/　　双人间（一张双人床）
18. twin room /twɪn//ruːm/　　双人标准间（两张单人床）
19. bath tub /bɑːθ//tʌb/　　浴缸
20. shower /'ʃaʊə/　　淋浴

Unit 6 Travel

Transportation

1. flight ticket /flaɪt/ /'tɪkɪt/ 机票
2. terminal /'tɜːmɪnəl/ 航站楼
3. airport check-in /'eəpɔːt/ /'tʃekɪn/ 机场登机手续办理处
4. carry-on luggage /'kærɪɒn/ /'lʌɡɪdʒ/ 随身行李
5. luggage /'lʌɡɪdʒ/ 行李
6. security /sɪ'kjʊərɪti/ 安检
7. boarding pass /'bɔːdɪŋ/ /pɑːs/ 登机牌
8. boarding gate /'bɔːdɪŋ/ /ɡeɪt/ 登机口
9. aisle /aɪl/ 过道
10. flight attendant /flaɪt/ /ə'tendənt/ 机舱乘务员
11. oxygen mask /'ɒksɪdʒən/ /mɑːsk/ 氧气面罩
12. emergency exit /ɪ'mɜːdʒənsi/ /'eksɪt/ 紧急疏散口
13. baggage claim /'bæɡɪdʒ/ /kleɪm/ 行李提取处
14. baggage carousel /'bæɡɪdʒ/ /ˌkærə'sel/ 行李传送带
15. schedule /'ʃedjuːl, 'skedʒuːl/ 时刻表
16. announcement /ə'naʊnsmənt/ 广播
17. ticket machine /'tɪkɪt/ /mə'ʃiːn/ 自动售（取）票机
18. destination /ˌdestɪ'neɪʃən/ 目的地
19. platform /'plætfɔːm/ 站台
20. train conductor /treɪn/ /kən'dʌktə/ 火车乘务员

Part II Sentence Patterns Related to Travel

1. **A:** You are English, aren't you?
   B: No, I'm Scottish.
2. **A:** Have you got a Scottish passport?
   B: No. I've got a British passport.

3. **A:** You would like a twin room with a shower, wouldn't you?
   B: No. We would like a double room with a bath tub.
4. **A:** Will you be staying for two nights?
   B: No. We'll be staying for three nights.

Section II   Conversations

You may want to communicate with people in English when you travel. Listen and learn the following conversations.

Conversation 1

A: Can I help you?
B: Yes, I've been booked on the flight to London. It's leaving in fifteen minutes.

A: Sorry, sir. This line is for Manchester. The London line is over there.
B: Oh, but I have been waiting in this line for half an hour.
A: Don't worry. The flight to London is delayed. You still have time.
B: Oh. Great!

Conversation 2

A: Madam. Is there a problem?
B: Yes. I was on flight AC32. The carousel for the flight has stopped and I don't see my bags.
A: Oh, too bad. Would you please fill out this report for your missing bags?
B: Sure. ... Will I be informed if you find my bags?

Unit 6 Travel

A: Yes. As soon as we find your bags, we'll call you and have them delivered to your hotel.
B: Good. Here is the finished form. Thank you.

Conversation 3

A: Next. Uh, your passport please.
B: OK.
A: Uh, what is the purpose of your visit?
B: I'm here to attend a medical conference, and then I plan on touring the city for a few days.
A: And where will you be staying?
B: I'll be staying at a hotel downtown for the entire trip.

Conversation 4

A: What do you have in your luggage?
B: Uh, well, just my personal belongings... clothes, scarves, shoes and a few books.
A: Okay. Please open your bag.
B: Sure.
A: Okay... Everything's fine. By the way, is this your first visit to the country?

B: Well, yes and no. Actually, I was born here when my parents were trying to finish their PhD research in a college in the city many years ago, but this is my first trip back since then.
A: Well, enjoy your stay.
B: Thanks.

Conversation 5

A: So, what do you want to do tomorrow?
B: Well, let's look at this city guide here. Uh, here's something interesting. Why don't we first visit the art museum in the morning?
A: OK. I like that idea. And where would you like to have lunch?

B: How about going to an Indian restaurant? The guide recommended one downtown a few blocks from the museum.

A: Great. After that, what do you think about visiting the zoo? It says here that there are some very unique animals not found anywhere else.

B: Sounds like a wonderful plan!

Section III　Practice

I. Complete the following conversation with the phrases given.

> A. you be travelling
> B. you would like to go
> C. you will be staying

A: I'd like to spend a few days in Singapore.

B: Can you tell me when 1_____?

A: Next month. Sometime after the 7th.

B: Fine. And could you tell me how long 2_____?

A: It depends on the price but preferably for four nights.

B: Well. We have some very good offers at the moment. Will 3_____ alone?

A: No, with my wife.

II. Complete the following conversation with the sentences given.

> A. but I'm really lost.
> B. And where do I get off the train?
> C. No problem.
> D. it's a hundred and thirty yen.
> E. Do you need any help?
> F. how often do the trains come around this time of day?

Unit 6

Travel

A: Let me see now. Which train do I need to get on?

B: Excuse me. 1_____

A: Yes, I want to go to Tokyo Tower, 2_____

B: First, you need to buy a ticket to your destination. From here, 3_____

A: A hundred and thirty yen. OK.

B: Then, get on the Hibiya Subway Line at Platform 4.

A: Number 4, alright. Oh, and 4_____

B: Usually, they come about every six minutes or so.

A: Alright. 5_____

B: Get off at Kamiyacho Station, three stops from here.

A: Three stops. Got it. Thanks for your help.

B: 6_____ Good luck.

III. Match the items in Column A with the items in Column B.

A	B
1. How much is the one-way fare?	A. It departs at 3:15 pm.
2. When does the plane leave tomorrow?	B. Oh, you're right. Sorry.
3. Could I get an aisle seat?	C. It costs $68.
4. Excuse me. I think you're in my seat.	D. Okay. What should I do?
5. I'm sorry, but that bag is too big to carry on the plane.	E. Sure. We have two available.

IV. Work in pairs and discuss the questions: Have you ever traveled to any of the following cities? Check the ones you have never visited but long to have a trip to and give your reasons.

★Lima, Peru

★Paris, France

★London, UK

★Vienna, Austria

★Rome, Italy

★Madrid, Spain

★Istanbul, Turkey

★Shanghai, China

★Tokyo, Japan

★Dubai, United Arab Emirates

V. Tell your partner what kind of travel you like best and what you want to do on your next trip.

There are many different kinds of travel, e.g. tours of safari, adventure, jungle, trekking, camping, cruising, general sightseeing, and seaside holiday etc.   Among them I like _____ the best, as it is the most _____ tour. This type of tour is _____ than the general type.

VI. Work in pairs and discuss the following questions.

★ Do you like travelling? Why or why not?

★ What do people benefit from their travel experiences?

★ Where do you want to travel on your next trip? Please explain your decision.

Unit 6 Travel

Section IV   Speaking Skills: Making Comparisons

You need to compare hotels when making a travel plan. Read the following expressions and learn how to make comparisons.

Comparing Hotels
The River Hotel is more expensive than the Crown Hotel.
The Western Hotel is the busiest hotel in this city.
The River Hotel is older than the Western Hotel.
Room prices here are as expensive as in other major cities.

Look at the information about the four hotels and work with a partner to compare them in number of rooms, facilities, location and comfort. Then select the best suitable one for different types of travelers, i.e. young students, shoppers, business travelers.

Hotel Names	A Double Room Price	Number of Rooms	Business Facilities	Good Restaurant	Close to Shops	Quiet Location	24-hour Room Service
the Youth Hotel	Under $100	121					
the Crown Hotel	$100-150	80	Yes				Yes
the Western Hotel	$100-150	22		Yes	Yes	Yes	
the River Hotel	$150-200	109	Yes	Yes			Yes

Section V Theme Extension

Part I Reading and Discussing

Read the following short passage and discuss the questions.

A violinist had been traveling round San Francisco as a member of a theater group. When the tour was over, she went to the airport and boarded the plane that would take her back home. She was in her seat, waiting for the plane to take off when she suddenly decided not to go after all. She rushed off the plane at the last minute, leaving the airline attendants thinking that she perhaps had planted a bomb on the plane and escaped. The plane and all the luggage was thoroughly searched by a bomb sniffing dog. Meanwhile, the airport police stopped her, and took her away to be questioned. However, after extensive questioning she managed to convince them that she had not planted a bomb: She simply couldn't bear to leave her new boyfriend! The plane was allowed to depart nearly four hours later, minus (减去) the love-struck violinist who then spent another two weeks in the states with the boyfriend.

Questions:
1. Which plane did the violinist board?
2. Why did the violinist suddenly decide not to go after all?
3. What did the airport police do then?
4. When did the plane finally depart from San Francisco?
5. Do you like the violinist in the story? Why or why not? Please give your reasons.

Unit 6 Travel

Part II Scenic Spots of the World

There are some special places which have their meanings and you have to see them to feel accomplished. The purpose is to make you love the nature which is called "the biggest wonder of the world".

1. Paris

Paris is the capital and most popular city of France, with an area of 105 square kilometers and a population of about 2.2 millions. Since the 17th century, Paris has been one of Europe's major centers of finance, commerce, fashion, science, music, and painting. According to a survey in 2018, Paris was the second-most expensive city in the world, behind Singapore.

Top attractions in Paris: the Notre Dame Cathedral, the Basilique du Sacré-Cœur on Montmartre, the Louvre Museum, the Eiffel Tower, Centre Pompidou, Musée d'Orsay, the City of Science and Industry, the Boat Tour of the Seine River, the Arc de Triomphe and the Champs-Elysees.

2. Rome

Rome is the capital city of Italy with about 2.9 million residents in 1,285 square kilometers. The Vatican City is an independent country inside the city boundaries of Rome, the only existing example of a country within a city. For this reason Rome has been often defined as capital of two states.

Top attractions in Rome: the Colosseum, the Pantheon, Vatican City, Rome Forum, Trevi Fountain, Centro Storico & the Spanish Steps, Piazza Navona, Borghese Gallery and Gardens.

3. Iceland

Iceland is an island country in the North Atlantic, with a population of about 350,000 and an area of 103,000 square kilometers, making it the most sparsely populated country in Europe. Iceland is volcanically and geologically active. You will see many mountains and glaciers in this country.

Top attractions in Iceland: Whale Watching in Reykjavik, Blue Lagoon in Grindavík, Strokkur Geysir, the Northern Lights, Maelifell Volcano & Myrdalsjökull Glacier Park, Skaftafell Ice Cave.

Describe a country or city you would like to visit on your next trip.

You should explain:

Why would you like to go there?

What is the best season to go there?

What is the most interesting thing to do there?

Then prepare a 2-minute oral report about this place and deliver it to your class.

Section VI   Rhythm Across the Sea

Listen to the following song and sing it with your friends.

Better Man

Send someone to love me	As my soul heals the shame
I need to rest in arms	I will grow through this pain
Keep me safe from harm	Lord I'm doing all I can
In pouring rain	To be a better man
Give me endless summer	
Lord I fear the cold	Go easy on my conscience
Feel I'm getting old	'Cause it's not my fault
Before my time	I know I've been taught

Unit 6

Travel

To take the blame
Rest assured my angels
Will catch my tears
Walk me out of here
I'm in pain
As my soul heals the shame
I will grow through this pain
Lord I'm doing all I can
To be a better man

Once U've found that lover you're homeward bound
Love is all around
Love is all around

I know some have fallen on stony ground
But Love is all around

Send someone to love me
I need to rest in arms
Keep me safe from harm
In pouring rain
Give me endless summer
Lord I fear the cold
Feel I'm getting old
Before my time
As my soul heals the shame
I will grow through this pain
Lord I'm doing all I can
To be a better man

SectionVII Pocket Poem

Appreciate the following poem and read it aloud.

Dreams
梦 想

Hold fast to dreams	紧紧抓住梦想
For if dreams die	梦想若是消亡
Life is a broken-winged bird	生命就像鸟儿折了翅膀
That can never fly	再也不能飞翔
Hold fast to dreams	紧紧抓住梦想
For when dreams go	梦想若是消丧
Life is a barren field	生命就像贫瘠的荒野
Frozen only with snow	雪覆冰封,万物不再生长

Unit 6 Travel

Section VIII Voice of Wisdom

You are going to listen to a famous speech. Listen carefully and try to imitate and read the passage out loud.

Turn off Your Phone and Discover All Human around Us

Graduation gives you the courage to be unreasonable. Don't bother to have a plan. Instead let's have some luck. Success is really about being ready for the good opportunities that come before you. It's not to have a detailed plan about everything you're going to do, you can't plan innovation or inspiration, but you can be ready for it. And when you see it, you can jump on it and you can make a difference, as many of the people here today have already done.

The important point here is, if you forego your plan you also then have to forego fear. In many ways in the last four years and maybe in high school as well, you've been penalized for making mistakes. From now on, the rewards will gravitate to those who make mistakes and learn from them, as the president said.

So stop right now. Take a minute and think of something completely new and go work on that. Take that as your challenge; take that as your opportunity. Whatever you care the most about.

So how should you do it, how should you behave? Well, do it in a group, its much more fun anyway. None of us is as smart as all of us. Universities now are good at teaching you how to work with other people, it's no longer the lone light sitting in the lab, it's a team.

And you can see Twitter as an example of a form of social intelligence, use it. Find a network of people that care about you and so forth and so on. You can imagine watching Watson and Crick, who discovered the structure of DNA, did it at a university.

You can imagine today, there are two people who probably met on Facebook at a university. And then are going to say to each other,

"What are you up to right now?" "Oh, I'm finding the secret of life, then I'm off to a pub. LOL." It's okay. Do it together.

But amidst all of this, some truths emerge. Leadership and personality matter a lot. Intelligence, education, and analytical reasoning matter. Trust matters. In the network world, trust is the most important currency.

Which brings me to my final question. What is, in fact, the meaning of life? And in a world where everything is remembered and everything is kept forever — the world you are in — you need to live for the future and the things that you really, really care about.

And what are those things? Well, in order to know that, I hate to say it, but you're going to have to turn off your computer. You're actually going to have to turn off your phone and discover all that is human around us.

You'll find that people really are the same all around the world. They really do care about the same things.

You'll find that curiosity and enthusiasm and passion are contagious. I see it with the students, I see it with the faculty, I see it with the trustees and the president here — it's contagious. Make it happen, take it with you.

You'll find that nothing beats holding the hand of your grandchild as he walks his first steps. You'll find that a mind set in its ways is a life wasted — don't do it.

You'll find that the resilience of a human being and the human spirit is amazing. You'll find today that the best chance you will ever have is right now, to start being unreasonable. But when you do, listen to me, be nice to your parents and true to your school.

Good luck, and thank you very much. Thank you.

Weather

Weather changes with four seasons. In spring it's warm with sunlight. In summer temperatures increase to their hottest of the year. Temperatures cool again and it's mild with soft breezes in autumn. It's cold with snow in winter. Some people say they like the weather with sunshine because sunny weather makes them happy. Does the weather really affect our moods? The fact is that in sorrow bad weather makes us feel depressed, while in joy we just remain high-spirited despite the bad weather. Actually there is no such thing as bad weather. Sunshine is sweet, rain is refreshing, wind braces us up, and snow is exhilarating. They're only different types of good weather.

Learning Objectives

In this unit you are going to:

★ learn some new words related to weather;

★ learn speaking skills — asking for information;

★ practice speaking around the topics given.

Section I Words and Sentence Patterns

Part I   Words Related to Weather

Weather talk is a way to pass the time or bridge a silence between strangers. Now let's discover the words and expressions about weather.

Land Sports

1.	sunny /'sʌnɪ/	晴
2.	cloudy /'klaʊdɪ/	多云
3.	overcast /ˌəʊvə'kɑːst/	天阴的
4.	rainy /'reɪnɪ/	下雨的
5.	drizzle /'drɪzəl/	毛毛雨
6.	shower /'ʃaʊə/	阵雨
7.	thunder storm /'θʌndə//stɔːm/	雷雨
8.	light rain /laɪt//reɪn/	小雨
9.	moderate rain /'mɒdərət//reɪn/	中雨
10.	heavy rain /'hevɪ//reɪn/	大雨
11.	snow /snəʊ/	雪
12.	snow shower /snəʊ//'ʃaʊə/	阵雪
13.	sleet /sliːt/	雨夹雪

Unit 7 Weather

14. hail /heɪl/ — 冰雹
15. blizzard /ˈblɪzəd/ — 大风雪
16. light snow /laɪt//snəʊ/ — 小雪
17. moderate snow /ˈmɒdərət//snəʊ/ — 中雪
18. heavy snow /ˈhevɪ//snəʊ/ — 大雪
19. windy /ˈwɪndɪ/ — 有风的
20. breeze /briːz/ — 微风
21. gale /geɪl/ — 大风
22. typhoon /taɪˈfuːn/ — 台风
23. hurricane /ˈhʌrɪkən/ — 飓风
24. haze /heɪz/ — 霾
25. foggy /ˈfɒgɪ/ — 有雾的
26. frost /frɒst/ — 霜冻
27. sandstorm /ˈsændstɔːm/ — 沙尘暴
28. visibility /ˌvɪzɪˈbɪlɪtɪ/ — 能见度
29. humidity /hjuːˈmɪdɪtɪ/ — 湿度
30. air pollution diffusion index /eə//pəˈluːʃən//dɪˈfjʊʒən//ˈɪndeks/ — 空气污染指数
31. centigrade /ˈsentɪgreɪd/ — 摄氏度
32. Fahrenheit /ˈfærənhaɪt/ — 华氏度

Part II Sentence Patterns Related to Weather

1. **A:** What will the weather be like next week?
   B: A blizzard is hitting us next Wednesday.
2. **A:** What will be the temperature tomorrow?
   B: It'll be 28℃.
3. **A:** What's the weather forecast for tomorrow?
   B: It says a storm may come tomorrow.

Section II Conversations

Who cares about the clouds when we're together? Just sing a song and bring the sunny weather. Listen and learn the following conversations.

Conversation 1

A: What's the weather forecast for the weekend?
B: It's going to rain on Saturday.
A: What about on Sunday?
B: It's getting worse.
A: Throughout the weekend?
B: I think so.

Conversation 2

A: Amy, what's the weather forecast for tomorrow?
B: It says a haze may come tomorrow.
A: Oh! I hate nasty hazy days!
B: Me, too! I always feel depressed on hazy days.
A: But quite often weather forecasts are not accurate. Maybe tomorrow is a clear day.
B: I hope so!

Conversation 3

A: The weather in Beijing is so lovely!
B: Autumn is the best time to visit Beijing.
A: Yes, I can see. The summer heat is gone. And the winter cold is still far behind.
B: What is the weather like in London at this time of the year?
A: Autumn is also very nice in London. Autumn days in London are crisp, cool and pleasant.

Unit 7 Weather

Conversation 4

A: Will the weather be good this weekend? What does the weather forecast say?
B: The weatherman says it's going to rain tomorrow.
A: Oh, no. I thought that we might go for a picnic.
B: It's really a pity. Is the gallery open at weekends?
A: Yes. Shall we go there?
B: OK. Good idea!
A: I like to visit libraries, museums and galleries on rainy days.
B: Why?
A: Sunny days bring out record crowds. But there are much fewer visitors on rainy days!

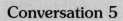

Conversation 5

A: How's the weather in your city today?
B: It's badly freezing. It snowed heavily all day and schools closed early.
A: What's the temperature?
B: It's -21℃ now. It was even colder this morning.
A: What's the weather going to be like tomorrow?
B: The news says it's probably going to clear up tomorrow.
A: I wish it would stay this way.
B: As long as it doesn't snow heavily.

Section III Practice

I. Complete the following conversation with the phrases given.

> A. it were summer
> B. watching the news
> C. pretty cold

A: Do you know what the weather is going to be like tomorrow?
B: I was 1_____ a little earlier.
A: What did they say?
B: They said it's probably going to snow tomorrow.
A: I really don't like the winter. I wish 2_____.
B: Me too. How's the weather where you are?
A: It's not too bad, but it's 3_____ here too. It was about 9℃ today and it rained heavily this afternoon.
B: Is it going to be warmer tomorrow?
A: I heard it's going to be a little warmer.

II. Complete the following conversation with the sentences given.

> A. The temperature has hit 98!
> B. What else can we do?
> C. I just hope it'll level off.
> D. I've never seen such scorching weather in my life!

A: Oh, my! It's really hot! 1_____
B: Tell me about it. It's like the whole world is broiling.
A: Oh, look at the thermometer! 2_____
B: I hope it's not going to break into three digits!
A: Well, 3_____
B: I guess we can't do anything until dark then.
A: I guess so. 4_____ We can't stay in the heat for long!

III. Match the items in Column A with the items in Column B.

A	B
1. Lovely day, isn't it?	A. It's such a nice change.
2. It seems to be clearing up.	B. Well, the worst of the winter should be over.
3. It's supposed to get cloudy and windy again this afternoon.	C. Yes, it's much better than yesterday.
4. It looks like it's going to be sunny.	D. Yes, it's not like what the radio said at all.

Unit 7 Weather

IV. Work in pairs and discuss the topic: Some people say weather affects our mood while others say weather doesn't have to impact our mood. What is your point of view towards these views? Give your reasons.

Weather affects our mood.	Weather doesn't have to impact our mood.
1.	1.
2.	2.
3.	3.
4.	4.
5.	5.

V. Tell your partner what you like to do best on rainy days and why.

On rainy days I usually _____. And I love doing it best because_____, _____, and _____.That's my special way of "remaining sunny" on rainy days!

VI. Work in pairs and discuss the following questions.
★ What are some examples of extreme weather?
★ Have you ever experienced extreme weather?
★ What is behind the extreme weather? Is it caused by global warming?

Section IV Speaking Skills: Asking for Information

How do people ask for information in English? Read the following expressions and learn a few skills.

Asking for Information
1. What's the weather like today?
2. How's the weather there today?

(continued)

Asking for Information
3. What will the weather be like tomorrow?
4. What's the temperature today?
5. What's the weather forecast for tomorrow?
6. What does the forecast say about the weekend?
7. Will it clear up tomorrow?
8. Will a bad rainstorm hit us next week?
9. Will the temperature go down steeply?
10. Is the heat wave coming to us?

Read the following passage. This weather personality type analysis was done only on Dutch teenagers about the weather in their country. Conduct a survey on how weather impacts your classmates' mood in our country. Discuss your findings with your partner.

The Impact of Weather May Depend on Your Weather Personality Type

Klimstra et al. (2011) found that half of the 415 adolescents studied weren't really impacted much at all by changes in the weather, while the other half were. Further analyses determined the following weather personality types:

Summer lovers (17 percent) — "Happier, less fearful, and less angry on days with more sunshine and higher temperatures. More hours of precipitation (降雨量) was associated with less happiness and more anxiety and anger."

Summer haters (27 percent) — "Less happy and more fearful and angry when the temperature and the percentage of sunshine were higher. With more hours of precipitation they tended to be happier and less fearful and angry."

Unit 7 Weather

Rain haters (9 percent) — "Angrier and less happy on days with more precipitation. By comparison, they were more happy and fearful, but less angry, on days with more sunshine and higher temperatures."

Unaffected by weather (47 percent) — Largely unimpacted by changes of the weather.

You can use the following questions for your survey.

1. How is the weather today?
2. Do you like the climate in our country?
3. What's your favorite season?
4. Does the change of seasons affect your mood? How?
5. What's your favorite kind of weather?
6. Is there any type of weather you really don't like?
7. Does heat wave make you more aggressive — or even more violent?
8. Does rain make you sad?
9. Does haze make you gloomy?
10. On cold winter days do you feel more like wanting to hibernate (冬眠), and isolate ourselves from others?

Section V Theme Extension

Part I Reading and Discussing

Read the following short passage and discuss the questions.

London is a city for all seasons, but possibly the most pleasant time of year to visit is Spring, which arrives usually in fits and starts (一阵一阵的) in early March, with some fresh, sunny days and the appearance of daffodils (水仙花) in the parks. Temperatures creep up through March and April until the daily average by mid-May is 17°C. Rainfall is relatively low in total during spring, but it comes in frequent showery bursts, making an umbrella and rain-coat useful accessories (配

饰). Look out for traditional spring time events like pancake races, fairs and festivals, and the Chelsea Flower Show.

Summer in London (June, July and August) is when the city's parks and gardens come into their own, providing green oases to escape the heat generated by the close-packed buildings and venues for a host of music festivals and other outdoor events, like the popular Notting Hill Carnival. Sunshine cannot be guaranteed, even in summer — drizzly, grey days are just as likely to occur as dry, sunny ones.

Autumn in London, from mid-September to November, is the wettest time of year. The days begin to shorten, and towards the end of October there is a definite nip (冷冻) in the air. Day time temperatures hover in the late teens (centigrade), beginning to drop into single figures in late October. Autumn days in London are crisp, cool and pleasant, with the added advantage that the summer crowds have dissipated (消散). September and October is trade exhibition and art fair season in London, with loads to see and do, indoors and out.

When winter closes in early December it becomes chilly and damp outdoors, with only an average hour a day of sunshine, but London's shops light up with Christmas decorations and the city takes on a festive air. The West End shows, top restaurants, music venues like the South Bank Centre and the O2, and London's cozy pubs and clubs draw the crowds in from out of the cold. Snowfall is rare in London, but expect plenty of intermittent (断断续续的) drizzle from December, through January.

Questions:

1. According to the passage, which season is the best time to visit London? Why?
2. What are useful accessories on rainy days in London?
3. What is the meaning of the phrase "the summer crowds have dissipated"(in Para 3)?
4. According to the passage, where can Londoners escape the heat in summer?
5. What is the weather like in winter in London? What can draw the crowds from out of the cold?

Unit 7 Weather

Part II Scenic Spots of the World

There are some special places which have their meanings and you have to see them to feel accomplished. The purpose is to make you love the nature which is called "the biggest wonder of the world".

1. New York

New York City is the largest and most populated city in the USA. It is often called the "city that never sleeps" because it is constantly buzzing with activity. The metropolis is the nexus (中心) of culture, art, architecture, history and entertainment. Many districts and landmarks in New York City are well known, with the city having the world's most visited tourist attractions.

Top attractions in New York: the Statue of Liberty, Empire State Building, Central Park, Times Square, the Brooklyn Bridge, Fifth Avenue, Rockefeller Center, Grand Central Terminal, the High Line, the National September 11 Memorial.

2. Vancouver

Vancouver is a coastal seaport city in western Canada, located in the Lower Mainland region of British Columbia. Vancouver is a relatively young metropolis, not even 200 years old, offering a wealth of Vancouver tourist attractions. Vancouver is one of the premier travel destination for its beaches, sprawling parks, snowy peaks setting the backstage for a nearly perfect vacation.

Top attractions in Vancouver: Capilano Suspension Bridge, Vancouver Aquarium, Stanley Park, Seawall Promenade, Gastown, Vancouver Lookout, University of British Columbia, Museum of Anthropology, Chinatown, Fort Langley Historic Site.

3. San Francisco

San Francisco is located at the tip of a peninsula between the San Francisco Bay and the Pacific coast. A compact city of steep rolling hills surrounded on three sides by water, San Francisco is renowned for its summer fogs, Victorian architecture, cable cars and beautiful vistas.

Top attractions in San Francisco: the Golden Gate Bridge, Fisherman's Wharf, Alcatraz, Golden Gate Park, Lombard Street, the Transamerica Pyramid, the Alamo Square, San Francisco's Chinatown, Palace of Fine Arts.

Describe an interesting place in your country that is not frequented by tourists.

You should say:

1. Where is it located?
2. Why is it interesting?
3. What can you do there?
4. Why do few people go there?

Section VI　Rhythm Across the Sea

Listen to the following song and sing it with your friends.

Love Story

We were both young when I first saw you. I closed my eyes and the flashback starts: I'm standing there on a balcony in summer air. See the lights, see the party, the ball gowns. See you make your way through the crowd and say hello.	Little did I know That you were Romeo; you were throwing pebbles. And my daddy said, "Stay away from Juliet." And I was crying on the staircase, begging you, "Please don't go."

Unit 7 Weather

And I said,

"Romeo, take me somewhere we can be alone."

I'll be waiting; all there's left to do is run.

You'll be the prince and I'll be the princess.

It's a love story, baby just say "yes."

So I sneak out to the garden to see you.

We keep quiet,'cause we're dead if they knew.

So close your eyes; escape this town for a little while.

'Cause you were Romeo, I was the scarlet letter,

And my daddy said, "Stay away from Juliet."

But you were my everything to me; I was begging you, "Please don't go."

And I said,

"Romeo, take me somewhere we can be alone."

I'll be waiting; all there's left to do is run.

You'll be the prince and I'll be the princess.

It's a love story, baby just say "yes."

Romeo save me; they try to tell me how I feel.

This love is difficult but it's real.

Don't be afraid; we'll make it out of this mess.

It's a love story, baby just say "yes."

I got tired of waiting,

Wondering if you were ever coming around.

My faith in you is fading

When I met you on the outskirts of town.

And I said,

"Romeo save me, I've been feeling so alone."

I keep waiting for you but you never come.

Is this in my head?

I don't know what to think.

He knelt to the ground and pulled out a ring and said,

"Marry me, Juliet. You'll never have to be alone.

I love you and that's all I really know.

I talked to your dad, go pick out a white dress."

It's a love story, baby just say "yes."

Oh oh, oh oh

'Cause we were both young when I first saw you

Section VII   Pocket Poem

Appreciate the following poem and read it aloud.

Trees
树

I think that I shall never see A poem lovely as a tree A tree whose hungry mouth is pressed Against the earth's sweet flowing breast; A tree that looks at God all day, And lifts her leafy arms to pray; A tree that may in summer wear A nest of robins in her hair; Upon whose bosom snow has lain; Who intimately lives with rain. Poems are made by fools like me, But only God can make a tree. 	我想，永远不会看到一首诗， 可爱的如同一株树一样。 一株树，她的饥渴的嘴 吮吸着大地的甘露。 一株树，她整日望着天 高擎着叶臂，祈祷无语。 一株树，夏天在她的发间 会有知更鸟砌巢居住。 一株树，白雪躺在她胸上， 她和雨是亲密的伴侣。 我这样的傻瓜可以作诗， 但只有上帝才能造树。 

Unit **7** Weather

Section VIII Voice of Wisdom

You are going to listen to a famous speech. Listen carefully and try to imitate and read the passage out loud.

What Can Adults Learn from Kids?

Now, I want to start with a question, when was the last time you were called childish? For kids like me, being called childish can be a frequent occurrence. Every time we make irrational demands, exhibit irresponsible behavior, or display any other signs of being normal American citizens, we are called childish. Which really bothers me. After all, take a look at these events: imperialism and colonization, world wars, George W. Bush, ask yourself: who is responsible? Adults.

Now, what have kids done? Well, Anne Frank touched millions with her powerful account of the Holocaust, Ruby Bridges helped end segregation in the United States, and most recently, Charlie Simpson helped to raise 120,000 pounds for Haiti on his little bike. So, as you can see evidenced by such examples, age has absolutely nothing to do with it. Childish addresses are seen so often in adults that we should abolish this age-discriminatory word when it comes to criticizing behavior associated with irresponsibility and irrational thinking.

Thank you.

Then again, who's to say that certain types of irrational thinking aren't exactly what the world needs? Maybe you have had grand plans before, but stopped yourself, thinking: "That's impossible", or "That costs too much", or "That won't benefit me". For better or worse, we kids aren't hampered as much when it comes to thinking about reasons why not to do things. Kids can be full of inspiring aspirations and hopeful thinking, like my wish that no one went hungry or that everything were free kind of Utopia. How many of you still dream like that and believe in the possibilities? Sometimes a

knowledge of history and the past failure of Utopia ideals can be a burden, because you know that if everything were free, that the food stocks would become depleted and scarce and lead to chaos. On the other hand, we kids still dream about perfection, and that's a good thing, because in order to make anything a reality, you have to dream about it first.

In many ways, our audacity to imagine helps push the boundaries of possibility. For instance, the museum of Glass in Tacoma, Washington, my home state — yoohoo Washington! — has a program called Kids Design Glass, and kids draw their own ideas for glass art. Now the resident artist said they got some of their best ideas through the program because kids don't think about the limitations of how hard it can be to blow glass into certain shapes. They just think of good ideas. Now when you think of glass, you might think of colorful Chihuly designs or maybe Italian vases. But kids challenge glass artists to go beyond that into the realm of broken-hearted snakes and bacon boys, who you can see has meat vision.

Now, our inherent wisdom doesn't have to be insiders' knowledge. Kids already do a lot of learning from adults, and we have a lot to share. I think that adults should start learning from kids. Now, I do most of my speaking in front of an education crowd, teachers and students, and I like this analogy, it shouldn't just be a teacher at the head of the classroom telling students do this, do that. The students should teach their teachers. Learning between grownups and kids should be reciprocal. The reality, unfortunately, is a little different, and it has a lot to do with trust, or a lack of it.

Now, if you don't trust someone, you place restrictions on them, right. If I doubt my older sister's ability to pay back the 10 percent interest I established on her last loan, I'm going to withhold her ability to get more money from me until she pays it back. True story, by the way. Now, adults seem to have a prevalently restrictive attitude towards kids from every "don't do that, don't do this" in the school handbook to restrictions on school Internet use. As history points out, regimes become oppressive when they are fearful about keeping control. And, although adults may not be quite of the level of totalitarian regimes, kids have no or very little, say in making the rules, when really the

Unit 7 Weather

attitude should be reciprocal, meaning that the adult population should learn and take into account the wishes of the younger population.

Now, what is even worse than restriction is that adults often underestimate kids abilities. We love challenges, but when expectations are low, trust me, we'll sink to them. My own parents had anything but low expectations for me and my sister. OK, so they didn't tell us to become doctors or lawyers or anything like that, but my dad did read to us about Aristotle and "pioneer germ fighters" when lots of other kids were hearing  "the wheels on the bus go round and round". Well, we heard that one too, but "pioneer germ fighters" totally rules.

I love to write from the age of four, and when I was six, my mom bought me my own laptop equipped with Microsoft Word. Thank you Bill Gates and thank you Ma. I wrote over 300 short stories on that little laptop, and I wanted to get published. Instead of just scoffing at this heresy that a kid wanted to get published, or saying wait until you are older, my parents were really supportive. Many publishers were not quite so encouraging. One large children's publisher ironically said that they didn't work with children. Children's publisher not working with children? I don't know, you are kind of alienating your clients there. Now, one publisher, Action Publishing was willing to take that leap and trust me and to listen to what I had to say, they published my first book, *Flying Fingers*, you see it here. And from there on, it has gone to speaking at hundreds of schools keynoting to thousands of educators, and finally, today, speaking to you.

 I appreciate your attention today because to show that you truly care, you listen. But there is a problem with this rosy picture of kids being so much better than adults. Kids grow up and become adults just like you. Or just like you? Really? The goal is not to turn kids into your kind of adult, but rather better adults than you have been, which maybe a little challenging considering your guys' credentials, but the way progress happens is because new generations and new eras grow and develop and become better than the previous ones. It's the reason we are not in the Dark Ages anymore. No matter what your position of

place in life, it's imperative to create opportunities for children so that we can grow up and blow you away.

Adults and fellow TEDsters, you need to listen and learn from kids and trust us and expect more from us. You must lend an ear today, because we are the leaders of tomorrow, which means we are going to be taking care of you when you are old and senile. No, just kidding. No, really, we are going to be the next generation, the ones who will bring this world forward. And in case you don't think that this really has meaning for you, remember that cloning is possible, that involves going through childhood again, in which case, you will want to be heard just like my generation. Now, the world needs opportunities for new leaders and new ideas. Kids need opportunities to lead and succeed. Are you ready to make the match? Because the world's problems shouldn't be the human family's heirloom.

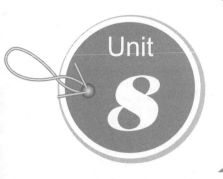

Festival

  A festival is an event ordinarily celebrated by a community and centering on some characteristics of that community and its religion or cultures. It is often marked as a local or national holiday. There are different kinds of festivals around the world, i.e. religious festivals, arts festivals, food and drink festivals, seasonal and harvest festivals. Many festivals are associated with harvest time such as Mid-autumn Festival and Halloween.

Learning Objectives

In this unit you are going to:
 ★ learn some new words related to festivals;
 ★ learn speaking skills — asking for and giving instructions;
 ★ practice speaking around the topics given.

Section I Words and Sentence Patterns

Part I Words Related to Festival

You may have learnt a lot about festivals. Do you know how to talk about festivals in English? Now let's learn some key words related to them.

Festivals (1)

1. festival /ˈfestɪvəl/ — 节日
2. event /ɪˈvent/ — 活动
3. celebrate /ˈselɪbreɪt/ — 庆祝
4. hold /həʊld/ — 举行
5. fall /fɔːl/ — 发生
6. observe /əbˈzɜːv/ — 庆贺
7. focus /ˈfəʊkəs/ — 要点
8. theme /θiːm/ — 主题
9. feature /ˈfiːtʃə/ — 以……为特色
10. community /kəˈmjuːnɪtɪ/ — 群体
11. ceremony /ˈserɪmənɪ/ — 仪式
12. parade /pəˈreɪd/ — 庆祝游行
13. legend /ˈledʒənd/ — 传奇
14. superstition /ˌsuːpəˈstɪʃən/ — 迷信
15. belief /bɪˈliːf/ — 宗教信仰
16. religion /rɪˈlɪdʒən/ — 宗教
17. associate with / əˈsəʊʃieɪt/wɪð/ — 与……相关
18. harvest /ˈhɑːvɪst/ — 丰收
19. fast /fɑːst/ — 斋戒
20. independence /ˌɪndɪˈpendəns/ — 独立

Unit 8 Festival

Festival (2)

1. origin /'ɒrɪdʒɪn/ — 起源
2. date back to — 追溯到……
3. commemorate /kə'meməreɪt/ — 纪念
4. remember /rɪ'membə/ — 记住
5. respect /rɪ'spekt/ — 尊敬
6. atmosphere /'ætməsfɪə/ — 气氛
7. serious /'sɪərɪəs/ — 严肃的
8. lively /'laɪvlɪ/ — 令人兴奋的
9. colorful /'kʌləfʊl/ — 多彩的
10. noisy /'nɔɪzɪ/ — 喧闹的
11. spectacular /spek'tækjʊlə/ — 壮观的
12. symbolize /'sɪmbəlaɪz/ — 象征
13. renewal /rɪ'njuːəl/ — 更新
14. reunion /ˌriː'juːnjən/ — 团聚
15. costume /'kɒstjuːm/ — 装束
16. homemade /ˌhəʊm'meɪd/ — 家里做的
17. feast /fiːst/ — 宴席
18. traditional /trə'dɪʃənəl/ — 传统的
19. annual /'ænjʊəl/ — 一年一度的
20. seasonal /'siːzənəl/ — 季节性的

Part II Sentence Patterns Related to Festival

1. **A:** When is the Singapore Art Week?
   B: Well, this annual celebration takes place in January to kick start the new year.
2. **A:** Where is this art festival held?
   B: It is held in galleries, museums, art precincts (区域) and independent art spaces.
3. **A:** Why is the festival celebrated?

B: To promote art appreciation to both Singapore residents and international visitors.

4. **A:** What does the art festival offer?

   B: It mainly offers visual arts, from traditional to modern to contemporary practices.

Section II   Conversations

You may want to be cool when communicating with your friends in English. Listen and learn the following conversations.

Conversation 1

A: How does your family celebrate Christmas?

B: We go sledding.

A: Sounds good. What else do you do?

B: We always go over to my grandparents' house and have dinner with them.

A: Well, that's great. Does your family eat anything particular for Christmas?

B: Turkey. We have turkey for every Christmas dinner.

Conversation 2

A: And what does Christmas mean to you?

B: Giving but not expecting to get.

A: Wow. That's quite something. But what does that mean: Giving but not expecting?

B: Well, we sneak up (悄悄来到) to the porch (门廊) of somebody that we want to give gift to. We put the gift, ring the doorbell, and hide.

A: So you're not expecting something; you just want to be generous to someone else. Is that right?

B: Yeah. That's correct.

Unit 8 Festival

Conversation 3

A: Could you please tell me something about Kwanzaa (宽扎节，非裔美国人的节日)?

B: Yes, of course. All our African-American communities celebrate it.

A: When do you celebrate it?

B: Well, Kwanzaa begins on December 26 and continues through January 1.

A: Oh, then what do people do to celebrate it?

B: Well, we give gifts and we light 7 candles, one each day.

Conversation 4

A: What public holidays do you have in the United States?

B: On the fourth Thursday of November we have a public holiday called Thanksgiving when people don't go to work. We traditionally spend the day with our family and have a large meal. Turkey and pumpkin pie are usually served.

A: Sounds great. Um, how did that idea begin?

B: Well, when the first settlers arrived at North America, they had great difficulties and the Indians taught and helped them a lot. After the first successful harvest, the settlers invited the Indians to a great feast. That's how it started.

Conversation 5

A: Tom invited me to the Highland Games but I know nothing about it.

B: Oh, you must go. It's very interesting!

A: Is it? Do you see sport games there?

B: Not only sport games. Well, some sport games are special and interesting, like throwing a heavy ball at the end of a chain and tossing the caber. And you are also bound to see many men wearing kilts (苏格兰褶裥短裙)…

A: Men wearing kilts?

B: Yes. Wearing kilts and playing music on bagpipes (风笛) and dancing!
A: Oh, I want to see that!
B: I bet you'll learn more about how Scottish and Celtic culture is celebrated there!

Section III Practice

I. Complete the following conversation with the phrases given.

> A. laughing all the time
> B. inviting me
> C. singing a famous song

A: Excuse me. What are they playing?
B: This violin playing is called "Liangzhu". It is the Chinese "Romeo and Juliet". It is about a love story.
A: It is beautiful. … What is the singer singing? Her voice is thrilling.
B: She is 1_____ — "My motherland".
A: What are the two men talking about? People are 2_____ but I cannot understand a single word!
B: Oh, it is called "comic crosstalk". Let me translate the talk for you.
A: Well, thank you for 3_____ to this Spring Festival Gala Show. I really enjoyed it.

II. Complete the following conversation with the given sentences.

> A. Who do you celebrate it with?
> B. What else do you do?
> C. Could you please tell me something about it?
> D. Does the name have any special meaning?
> E. When do you celebrate it?

A: I'm expected to deliver a report about Diwali. 1_____
B: Yes. …It's celebrated throughout India, as well as in Hindu communities in other countries.

Unit 8 Festival

A: 2_____

B: It falls around the end of October and the beginning of November.

A: 3_____

B: Yes. It is also known as the "festival of lights". In other words, it symbolizes the renewal of life.

A: 4_____

B: Well, the festival is a time for family reunion. Children give each other sweets and everybody lets off fireworks.

A: Interesting. 5_____

B: Uh, it's common to wear new clothes and jewelry on the first day of the festival, clean the house and open all the windows.

A: Oh, I must go and join you for the next Diwali! I like lights and new clothes! Thank you very much!

III. Match the items in Column A with the items in Column B.

A	B
1. What time does the party start?	A. About 15 people are coming.
2. How many are coming to the party?	B. Thanks. It was fun to make.
3. Should I bring something to the party?	C. That's a great idea.
4. Wow. This New Year rice cake is great.	D. It begins at 7:00 pm.
5. Hey. Let's play some games.	E. It would be great if you could get a bottle of wine.

IV. Work in pairs and discuss the questions: Choose a country you want to learn about and study more — What is the name of the country? What unique activities do people take part in to celebrate the New Year? What special clothes do people wear? What special food do people eat? Do people give or send any special gifts to family members and friends? If so, describe them.

★China

★Japan

★India

★Brazil

★Republic of Korea

★Greece

★Denmark

★Russia

★Belgium

★Canada

V. Tell your partner what New Year's resolution you made and how you are doing with it or what resolution you probably want to make.

My New Year's resolution is to _____ in order to _____ because _____ _____. I'm doing _____ with my resolution and I believe _____.

VI. Work in pairs and discuss the following questions.

★ Among all the Chinese festivals, which one do you like best?
★ What special features does it have?
★ What cultural and historical background does this festival have?

Section IV Speaking Skills: Asking for and giving instruction

There are many ways of asking for and giving instructions. Read the following expressions and learn a few of them.

Unit 8

Festival

Asking for Instructions	Giving Instructions
How do I …?	Before you begin, you should…
Could you show me how to…?	The first thing you do is…
Do you know how to…?	I would start by…
How do I go about?	After that, …
What do you suggest?	The next step is to…
What is the first step?	Once you've done that, then…
What's next?	In the end, …
And then?	When you've finished, …
What is the best way to…?	When you've completed all the steps, …

Interview 5 classmates by using the following form to find out the festival food that each of them likes best. Then ask each of them to explain to you how to make the food, using the expressions listed above.

Festival Food	Dumplings	Tangyuan (Glutinous Rice Balls)	Zongzi (Glutinous Rice Dumpling)	Mooncake
Student 1				
Student 2				
Student 3				
Student 4				
Student 5				

Section V Theme Extension

Part I Reading and Discussing

Read the following short passage and discuss the questions.

Long, long ago, there were ten suns in the sky. The suns burnt all the plants and people were dying on Earth. One day, excellent archer Hou Yi used his bow and arrows and shot down nine of the suns and Earth was saved.

The Western Queen Mother gave Hou Yi a bottle of elixir that could make a person immortal. Then one of Hou Yi's students tried to seize the elixir when Hou Yi wasn't at home. Faced with this greedy student, Chang'e, Hou Yi's wife decided to drink the elixir. It made her fly to the moon where she would stay forever.

On the night of the Mid-Autumn Festival, when the moon is bright, children like to try their best to find the shape of Chang'e on the moon.

Questions:
1. What other images on the moon do people often try to find?
2. Have you heard about Wu Gang and the Jade Rabbit? What stories do you know about them?
3. Explain to your partner how you and your family celebrate the Mid-Autumn Festival.

Part II Scenic Spots of the World

There are some special places which have their meanings and you have to see them to feel accomplished. The purpose is to make you love the nature which is called

Unit 8 Festival

"the biggest wonder of the world".

1. Sydney

Sydney is the state capital of New South Wales, Australia. It is located on Australia's east coast. Sydney is made up of 658 suburbs, 40 local government areas and 15 contiguous regions. Residents of the city are known as "Sydneysiders". As of June 2017, Sydney's estimated population was 5,131,326. Despite being one of the most expensive cities in the world, Sydney ranks the tenth in the world in terms of quality of living, as one of the most livable cities.

Top attractions in Sydney: Sydney Opera House, Sydney Harbor Bridge, the Rocks, Circular Quay, Darling Harbor, the Royal Botanic Garden, Sydney Tower, Queen Victoria Building and Art Gallery of New South Wales.

2. The South Island

The South Island is the larger of the two major islands of New Zealand, the other being the smaller North Island. The South Island covers 150,437 square kilometers, making it the world's 12th-largest island. It has a temperate climate. Tourism is a huge earner for the South Island. Popular tourist activities include sightseeing, adventure tours such as glacier climbing and bungee jumping, tramping (hiking), kayaking, and camping. Numerous walking and hiking paths such as the Milford Track, have huge international recognition.

Top attractions in the South Island: Fiordland National Park, Abel Tasman National Park, Westland National Park, Aoraki/Mount Cook National Park, Queenstown, Kaikoura and the Marlborough Sounds.

3. The Great Barrier Reef

The Great Barrier Reef is the world's largest coral reef system and is located in the Coral Sea, off the coast of Queensland, Australia. The Great Barrier Reef can be seen from outer space and is

the world's biggest single structure made by living organisms. It was selected as a World Heritage Site in 1981. CNN labeled it one of the seven natural wonders of the world.

Top attractions in the Great Barrier Reef: Cairns, the Whitsundays, Green Island and Lady Elliot Island.

Describe an activity you would like to participate in with friends.

You should say:

Where would you like to go?

What interesting activities are available there?

What exercise and equipment do you need for it?

Then explain who you would like to go there with.

Section VI　　Rhythm Across the Sea

Listen to the following song and sing it with your friends.

Last Christmas

Last Christmas	Once bitten and twice shy
I gave you my heart	I keep my distance
But the very next day you gave it away	But you still catch my eye
This year	Tell me, baby
To save me from tears	Do you recognize me?
I'll give it to someone special	Well, it's been a year
	It doesn't surprise me
Last Christmas	
I gave you my heart	Happy Christmas
But the very next day you gave it away	
This year	I wrapped it up and sent it
To save me from tears	With a note saying "I love you."
I'll give it to someone special	I meant it

Unit 8 Festival

Now I know what a fool I've been
But if you kissed me now
I know you'd fool me again

Last Christmas
I gave you my heart
But the very next day you gave it away
This year
To save me from tears
I'll give it to someone special

Last Christmas
I gave you my heart
But the very next day you gave it away
This year
To save me from tears
I'll give it to someone special

A crowded room
Friends with tired eyes
I'm hiding from you
And your soul of ice
My god, I thought you were
Someone to rely on
Me?

I guess I was a shoulder to cry on
A face on a lover with a fire in his heart
A man under cover, but you tore me apart
Now I've found a real love you'll never fool me again

Last Christmas
I gave you my heart
But the very next day you gave it away
This year
To save me from tears
I'll give it to someone special

Last Christmas
I gave you my heart
But the very next day you gave it away
This year
To save me from tears
I'll give it to someone special

A face on a lover with a fire in his heart
A man under cover, but you tore him apart

I'll give it to someone special
I'll give it to someone special

Section VII Pocket Poem

Appreciate the following poem and read it aloud.

What Is Time?
什么是时间？

Time is grain for peasants.	对农民来说，时间就是粮食。
Time is wealth for workers.	对工人来说，时间就是财富。
Time is life for doctors.	对医生来说，时间就是生命。
Time is victory for soldiers.	对军人来说，时间就是胜利。
Time is knowledge for students.	对学生来说，时间就是知识。
Time is speed for scientists.	对科学家来说，时间就是速度。
Time is money for enterprisers.	对企业家来说，时间就是金钱。
Time is everything for all of us.	对我们大家来说，时间就是一切。
Therefore, seize this day!	因此，把握今天！
Begin now!	现在就开始！
Each day is a new life.	每天都是一次新生。
Seize it. Live it.	把握住它，好好生活。
For today already walks tomorrow.	因为今天未逝时，明天已开始。

Unit 8 Festival

Section VIII Voice of Wisdom

You are going to listen to a famous speech. Listen carefully and try to imitate and read the passage out loud.

Adults, Please, Make Your Actions Reflect Your Worlds

Hello, I'm Severn Suzuki speaking for E.C.O. — the Environmental Children's Organization. We are a group of twelve and thirteen year-olds from Canada trying to make a difference: Vanessa Suttie, Morgan Geisler, Michelle Quigg and me. We raised all the money ourselves to come six thousand miles to tell you adults you must change your ways. Coming here today, I have no hidden agenda. I am fighting for my future.

Losing my future is not like losing an election or a few points on the stock market. I am here to speak for all generations to come.

I am here to speak on behalf of the starving children around the world whose cries go unheard.

I am afraid to go out in the sun now because of the holes in the ozone. I am afraid to breathe the air because I don't know what chemicals are in it.

I used to go fishing in Vancouver with my dad until just a few years ago we found the fish full of cancers. And now we hear about animals and plants going extinct every day — vanishing forever.

In my life, I have dreamt of seeing the great herds of wild animals, jungles and rainforests full of birds and butterflies, but now I wonder if they will even exist for my children to see.

Did you have to worry about these little things when you were my age?

All this is happening before our eyes and yet we act as if we have all the time we want and all the solutions. I'm only a child and I don't have all the solutions, but I want you to realise, neither do you!

You don't know how to fix the holes in our ozone layer. You don't know how to bring salmon back up a dead stream. You don't know how to bring back an animal now extinct. And you can't bring back forests that once grew where there is now desert. If you don't know how to fix it, please stop breaking it!

Here, you may be delegates of your governments, business people, organizers, reporters or politicians — but really you are mothers and fathers, brothers and sister, aunts and uncles — and all of you are somebody's child.

I'm only a child yet I know we are all part of a family, five billion strong, in fact, 30 million species strong and we all share the same air, water and soil — borders and governments will never change that.

I'm only a child yet I know we are all in this together and should act as one single world towards one single goal.

In my anger, I am not blind, and in my fear, I am not afraid to tell the world how I feel.

In my country, we make so much waste, we buy and throw away, buy and throw away, and yet northern countries will not share with the needy. Even when we have more than enough, we are afraid to lose some of our wealth, afraid to share.

In Canada, we live the privileged life, with plenty of food, water and shelter — we have watches, bicycles, computers and television sets. The list could go on for two days.

Two days ago here in Brazil, we were shocked when we spent some time with some children living on the streets. And this is what one child told us: "I wish I was rich and if I were, I would give all the street children food, clothes, medicine, shelter and love and affection."

If a child on the street who has nothing, is willing to share, why are we who have everything still so greedy?

I can't stop thinking that these children are my age, that it makes a tremendous difference where you are born, that I could be one of those children living in the Favellas of Rio; I could be a child starving in Somalia; a victim of war in the Middle East or a beggar in India.

I'm only a child yet I know if all the money spent on war was spent on ending poverty and finding environmental answers, what a wonderful place this earth would be!

At school, even in kindergarten, you teach us to behave in the world. You teach us: not to fight with others, to respect others, to clean up our mess, not to hurt other creatures, to share — not be greedy.

Then why do you go out and do the things you tell us not to do?

Do not forget why you're attending these conferences, who you're doing this for — we are your own children. You are deciding what kind of world we will grow up in. Parents should be able to comfort their children by saying "everything's going to be alright", "we're doing the best we can" and "it's not the end of the world".

But I don't think you can say that to us anymore. Are we even on your list of priorities? My father always says, "You are what you do, not what you say."

Well, what you do makes me cry at night. You grown ups say you love us. I challenge you, please make your actions reflect your words. Thank you for listening.